PREFACE
Lisa's Testimonial

It's hard to believe it's been almost thirty years since my food allergies and overgrowth of candida forced me to change my diet. Allergic to gluten, peanuts, and dairy, most days it felt like I was living in a pinball machine. My emotions and energy would suddenly crash; my brain and eyes would get foggy; my fingers and throat would swell, my nose would run, my joints would ache…I thought it was all just a part of getting older! But thirty years old is still young, and what I was experiencing were all allergic reactions.

Further complicating things, after being diagnosed with bad digestion by my chiropractor and undergoing a series of tests by assorted allergists and naturopaths, I discovered that I was also suffering from an overgrowth of candida. Candida is an overgrowth of yeast that can be caused by stress, birth control pills, and/or antibiotics, and I experienced twenty-six out of forty candida symptoms. For example: if it was dark and rainy out, conditions which promote the growth of mold, I would feel tired and down. If it was a sunshiny day, I would be up emotionally upbeat and energetic.

Suddenly, my dietary options were much fewer. The allergist told me I could either take a bunch of drugs and continue eating the way I had been for the past thirty years, or I could change my diet.

I chose to change my diet, and it's the best decision I ever made. Despite the allergist's recommendation that I take the pharmaceutical route, treating my allergies with drugs and medication, I know that modern medicine doesn't always get to the heart of our health challenges. Too often, they're content to throw drugs at everything, treating the symptoms without even trying to find the cause.

And so, I chose to clean out my cupboards of everything I was allergic to, taking the first steps on what has been a decades-long journey to better food and wellness. And I *was* feeling better. Not just better—I felt *great!* I was alive, vibrant, and dynamic. I wanted to shout it from the rooftops. As I started to "come back to life," I became very passionate about the positive effects changing my diet had had. I started taking a ton of classes on how food can affect your health; I spent my vacation days getting certified as a Health Coach at the Institute of Integrative Nutrition in New York City; I got certified as an Associate Raw Chef Instructor at the Living Light Culinary Institute of Raw Foods at Ft. Bragg in California; I even got certified in permaculture and herbalism.

I was on a journey, seeking and finding new ways to use food to reach higher standards of living. My food journey took me from eating microbiotic, to vegetarian, and ultimately to living a predominantly raw lifestyle. And this wasn't a planned journey; it just evolved as I went along with the flow of things. It's like going from one stepping stone to the next. I remember having lunch years ago with my then-Senior Design Manager, and I said, "I've come to the conclusion that I'm vegetarian. The only time I eat meat is when I'm a guest in someone's home!" His only response was to say, "I know." I hadn't even realized it! From that conversation on, I never ate meat again. I remember spending that whole week on cloud nine, enjoying a new euphoria and energy I'd never experienced before. I even had the best game of golf I've ever played!

Part of sharing my eating journey with others is a lot of myth busting. People ask, "Where do you get your protein if you don't eat meat?" What too many people don't know is, there is protein in everything! Did you know there is more

The 30-Day Program for Eating Healthier and Improving Your Diet with Vegan Foods

VEGAN

CHALLENGE

LISA MONTGOMERY
Foreword by Catherine Gill

hatherleigh

Hatherleigh Press is committed to preserving and protecting the natural resources of the earth. Environmentally responsible and sustainable practices are embraced within the company's mission statement.

Visit us at www.hatherleighpress.com and register online for free offers, discounts, special events, and more.

VEGAN CHALLENGE

Interior images provided courtesy of
WRawP, The Dirty Vegan, and Tribest Co.

COVER AND INTERIOR DESIGN BY CAROLYN KASPER

Printed in the United States
10 9 8 7 6 5 4 3 2 1

CONTENTS

protein in broccoli, kale, and spinach then meat? Plus, it's easily assimilated. "How do you get sugar in your body so your brain stays lit up?" Answer: fruits are a great resource.

My eating journey also affected my life socially. In addition to attending all the healthy cooking classes, where I got to meet so many new and wonderful people, I also started monthly raw potlucks in my home with local and world-renowned guest speakers.

At the same time, I also started a raw potluck newsletter. As a result of that newsletter, Carol Alt's co-writer on *The Raw 50* reached out to me, wanting to include some of the recipes from my raw potluckers in her book. This recipe request snowballed into my first of many wellness expos, with Carol Alt as our first guest speaker. It's crazy to think how just changing my diet could also change my life.

When my first book came out in 2009, I shared it with my general practitioner, who pronounced me the healthiest person in his practice of 3,600 patients. "If everyone ate like you, exercised, and got their rest, they wouldn't need me!" he said. Two years ago, I said to him, "You know, doc, I quote you a lot when people ask me why I eat healthy." I reminded him of what he'd said in 2009, to which he replied, "Lisa, my practice is now 10,000 strong, and you are *still* the healthiest person in it. You are in a class by yourself!"

In addition to feeling better physically, I had also grown emotionally and spiritually. Let' s face it: if you feel like a slug and can barely make it through the day and all you want to do is crash, you're not going to care about growing as a person. As I got healthier, I started exercising more frequently, which only improved my outlook. It was exercise that saved me, back before I learned I had food allergies. My immune system would have been impacted even more if I hadn't committed to exercising regularly and getting my rest. Then, last year, I left my stressful and degrading day job and my bully of a boss, which meant

I had a lot more energy to put towards staying positive and upbeat. Stress is emotionally draining, just like eating unhealthy food is physically draining. So as soon as I could financially afford to leave, I took off and have never once looked back. It was one of the best things I ever did.

I am now enjoying a type of freedom—physically, emotionally, spiritually, and financially—that I had never dreamed of. These are beautiful gifts; until I obtained it for myself, I had no idea how blessed life could be.

Another gift we all too often take for granted is our health…until we lose it. Bad health, whether it's a cold or a broken leg, affects your overall being. A few years ago, I broke my ankle and had to use crutches for three months. I couldn't take a shower during that time and was forced to wash my hair in the kitchen sink and take washcloth baths. I had to go up and down the stairs sitting on my butt. When I took my first shower after three months, I actually cried.

The little things in life are the special gifts—from sunrises and sunsets, a baby smiling, burping, sneezing…okay, anything a baby does is adorable. The neat thing about leaving corporate America and being in charge of my own path is I get to be present in my life, instead of just passing through it. I can fully enjoy going out to the back lawn with the dogs, bees, and chickens. I can breathe in the fresh air, feel the breeze.

We only have so much time on this planet, and it goes by so quickly. I know we have all heard it, but now that I'm sixty-one (wasn't I just twenty-nine yesterday?), you realize how quickly time flies by. You don't want to spend half of your life in a hospital because you made poor food and lifestyle choices. I've watched family members make some really bad food and lifestyle choices, and they're no longer with us. The last years of their lives were physically and emotionally stressful for them and for those they left behind, all because of those poor lifestyle choices.

You may feel that eating healthy, getting to the gym, and getting your rest is just too much on top of your already overburdened schedule, or you don't want to give up the vices you feel are oh-so-important. But it might just be time to re-evaluate your life and decide for yourself what is *really* important. If you aren't healthy, you won't have the opportunity to participate in all the activities that you find are important. I watched my oldest sister, a Retired Colonel in the USAF with a genius IQ, as her liver, kidney, and heart shut down after a life of alcoholism. She died within moments of her life support machines being turned off. And I was the one who had to pull the plug. Ironically, it was the person with a genius IQ who died, brain dead and an alcoholic, on New Year's Day.

If you don't want to put your loved ones through that or don't want to go through something like that yourself, I implore you to start changing your life today.

"*I was breathing, but I wasn't alive.*" This is a line from a chorus that we sang in my church last weekend. It really hit home for me; it felt like a perfect description of me before changing my diet. Once I healed my body physically I was better able to become present emotionally and spiritually. Leaving my day job, with its toxic management and long, stressful hours, has also allowed me to be present and alive in my own life.

Life is about choices. I choose to live dynamically.

Which life do you choose?

> "*Sometimes the most insanely great thing God will ever do in our lives will be the change He makes in us, not what He accomplishes through us.*"
> —BRIAN JONES, author of *Finding Favor: God's Blessings Beyond Health, Wealth, and Happiness*

FOREWORD
by Catherine Gill, the "Dirty Vegan"

It should come as no surprise that recent research has proven that a vegan diet is the ultimate trifecta—veganism benefits the environment, is healthiest for the human body, *and* is the most compassionate choice for animals, who are seen as merely products in the food industry.

As a vegan expert, author, and holistic chef myself, I have personally benefited from living a plant-based life. The wholeness and vigor that I relish in today, my excellent health and well-being, I attribute entirely to eating vegan. I am proof that it works; many of my bothersome ailments, as well as a chronic digestive condition, were alleviated through my lifestyle change to this healthier way of eating. It was to share this healing message that I first started my blog, The Dirty Vegan.

I am proud of what my colleague, Lisa Montgomery, is doing here with *Vegan Challenge* because, as living proof that a plant-based diet is best, I am certain that when done correctly, with thoughtful execution, a raw vegan diet can do so many wonderful things for your mind, body and spirit. I myself love to include raw foods as much as possible in my diet; over the years, many health and nutrition experts have not only advocated for, but lived their best lives because they included, as much raw produce as possible. For instance, my very own friend, Patricia Bragg, is a prime example of the wonderful raw and holistic results that can be gained through following a plant-based nutrition plan. By following the principles in *Vegan Challenge*, you too can delight in good health and longevity, just as we accomplished professionals in the holistic field and our predecessors have.

Lisa is a Certified Health Coach, a Raw Foods Chef and a Natural Foods Expert with over 30 combined years' experience studying her own health and the relationship that food plays to restorating one's physical condition and healing from illness. Who better than someone who has overcome her own health challenges and who now lives a better, more healthful life to show the way towards a more wholesome and supportive nutrition plan?

Lisa's personal health journey and the work that she has done over the years in the natural community is so inspiring that I have no doubt that you will be touched and motivated to improve your own health as well. I am proud of the Vegan Challenge for everything that it has to offer to the entire world—to you, and your health as a human being; to the animals that deserve respect and compassion; and to our planet, which benefits so greatly from the vegan lifestyle.

To wellness, inside and out!

—CATHERINE GILL, Author of *The Dirty Vegan Cookbook*

INTRODUCTION

Why am I, a person who advocates for a raw food lifestyle, writing a book about challenging yourself to live vegan?

Whenever I would share about healthy living, whether it be on the radio, TV, in articles and books, or during workshops, the common response was always that a predominantly raw food diet was, for many people, too limiting and too hard to sustain. Many people say it is easier to make healthy food choices in the warm summer months because of the warm temperatures, long days, and an abundance of fresh fruits and vegetables. On top of that, the cold temperatures of the winter months are a tough time to live the raw food lifestyle, when you want to eat piping hot foods to bring some warmth back into your body.

While there are options to counter each of these issues—modern grocery stores can supply fresh fruits and vegetables year-round like never before, and making warming soups is well within the scope of eating raw—the simple fact is that the word "raw" scares many people away.

I decided to write *Vegan Challenge* for the same reason I wrote *Raw Challenge*: to help people start eating and living healthier. Regardless of the specifics of your diet, if you want to see positive changes in your body—whether it be weight loss, increased energy, better mood, etc.—eliminating all processed foods, white flour, sugar, glutens, dairy, caffeine, and recreational stimulants (drugs and/or alcohol) is a great place to start. I realize it may sound daunting at first, but by taking baby steps and eliminating the foods that are tearing down your health and strengthening it with food that will build up your body, you will start to feel better right away.

When I held my "Raw Challenge" workshops at Kimberton Whole Foods in Pennsylvania a few years ago, within the first week, the participants were feeling better and sleeping better; they'd lost weight and their skin had that healthy lifestyle glow. It all goes to show the immense benefits that taking even that first positive step can have on your whole life.

The biggest challenge is overcoming your own brain. If it's anything like mine, your brain is your worst enemy. Telling you, "It can't be done," or "You're missing out, and don't those cookies just taste sooo good?" So, instead of thinking about what you *think* you are giving up, think about the exciting new life that you never dreamed was possible. When I first changed my diet, words like "sprouts," "quinoa," and "spirulina" were completely unknown to me. I didn't even know how to pronounce them, let alone prepare them. Start by just adding one new healthy dish/meal a week, and in no time, you'll have opened yourself to a whole new way of life. Try it with a smoothie for breakfast and do nothing else for that month but just drink the smoothie for breakfast. Once you've got that down, then try introducing a new side dish at dinner. Or, instead of packaged wheat or white flour pasta, try spiralizing some zucchini. If you aren't feeling that adventurous, there are pre-made black bean and mung bean pastas.

The point is to let your imagination run wild. If you have a family and want to make these healthy changes together, it's even easier, because you can make planning healthy meals a family event. Make it fun; make it a group activity. You never know, it just might be a way for families to come together at dinner time, like my family did when I was growing up.

Soon you'll find that making these healthy choices is easy, even obvious. During my food journey, I found that my taste buds had changed, so that what

I used to think tasted good—the cookies, cakes, and diet sodas—no longer held any appeal for me. I no longer even *wanted* those unhealthy options. On those rare occasions where I would listen to my darker impulses and succumb to ice cream with a cookie chaser, I found it didn't taste nearly as good as I remembered. Even worse, unhealthy food now made me sick! Turns out eating healthy agrees with me.

In this book, we have provided a huge assortment of vegan recipes for breakfast, lunch, and dinner to help you get started on your own personal vegan challenge. Pick and choose what recipes work for you or use what we have provided to inspire you and your family to create your own recipes. Remember: it takes as little as three weeks to create and keep a change, so don't give up! Stay committed to making today the best day of your life.

Remember, our thoughts become our actions, which then become our lifestyle. Look at the positives, focus on how far you've come. If it took you however long to wear your body down, it's going to take some time to build your body back up. But you *will* feel better, and you *will* thank yourself for it.

HOW TO FOLLOW THE VEGAN CHALLENGE

We've broken this book down into three sections to make it even easier for you to take this first step and make a positive change towards a healthier lifestyle.

In this first section, you will find an overview of what the vegan diet involves, along with a discussion of the many health benefits of a vegan diet. I've also included guidance on what you can expect during and after your Vegan Challenge, as well as helpful tips and tricks to aid you on your journey.

Following that, you'll find the Challenge itself, built to make you feel like I am right there with you, holding your hand the whole way. You will find entries for each of the thirty days in your Vegan Challenge. Each day comes complete with meal suggestions for Breakfast, Lunch, and Dinner, using the recipes which make up the bulk of this book. Each day also includes journaling space for you to add your own notes and experiences.

Finally, we've included over 100 wonderful recipes to choose from, all of them 100 percent vegan and 100 percent delicious! We hope you enjoy these recipes as much as we enjoyed creating them. If you are newly vegan, start by trying out some of these delicious dishes. Once you feel comfortable making vegan meals, let your creativity run wild!

I know you can do it, and you should, too. I did it, and if I can do it—anyone can change their life around. So, let's get started on your very own Vegan Challenge, and start the next chapter of your healthier life!

WHAT TO EXPECT FROM YOUR VEGAN CHALLENGE

WHAT IS VEGANISM?

Merriam-Webster describes veganism as a diet which restricts food products that come from animals, such as meat, eggs, or dairy products, and an associated philosophy that rejects the commodity status of animals. A follower of either the diet or the philosophy is known as a vegan. (Some vegans also abstain from using animal products such as leather.)

This is different from a vegetarian; Merriam-Webster defines a vegetarian as a person who does not eat meat, and whose diet consists wholly of vegetables, fruits, grains, nuts, and occasionally eggs or dairy products.

There are variations of vegetarianism: an ovo-lacto vegetarian diet includes both eggs and dairy products; an ovo-vegetarian diet includes eggs but not dairy products; and a lacto-vegetarian diet includes dairy products but not eggs. Semi-vegetarian diets are those which consist largely of vegetarian foods but may include fish or poultry, and occasionally other meats on an infrequent basis. Those with diets containing fish or poultry may define meat only as mammalian flesh and may therefore identify with vegetarianism. A pescatarian diet, for example, has been described as a diet of "fish but no other meat."

A well-planned vegan diet can reduce the risk of some types of chronic disease, including heart disease. It is regarded as appropriate for all stages of the life, including during infancy and pregnancy, by the American Academy of Nutrition and Dietetics, Dietitians of Canada, and the British Dietetic Association.

Donald Watson coined the term "vegan" in 1944 when he co-founded the Vegan Society in England. At first it was used to mean a "non-dairy vegetarian," but from 1951 onwards, the society defined itself as following "the doctrine that man should live without exploiting animals." Interest in veganism increased in the 2010s as more vegan stores opened and vegan options became increasingly available in supermarkets and restaurants in many countries.

RAW FOODISM

Raw foodism is the dietary practice of eating only or mostly uncooked, unprocessed foods. Depending on the philosophy or type of lifestyle and results desired, raw food diets may include a selection of fruits, vegetables, nuts, seeds, eggs, fish, meat, and dairy products. It may include simply processed foods such as various types of sprouted seeds, cheese, and fermented foods such as yogurts, kefir, kombucha, or sauerkraut, but generally not foods that have been pasteurized or homogenized.

A raw vegan diet consists of predominantly raw plant foods that have not been heated above 104–118°F. The premise is that foods cooked above this temperature have lost much of their nutritional value and are less healthy or even harmful to the body.

MODERN HEALTHY OPTIONS

When I changed my diet almost thirty years ago, the only place I could find organic and/or healthy options was Kimberton Whole Foods (a local northwest Philadelphia store) and Whole Foods Markets. Today, virtually all grocery stores have organic produce and a natural products aisle. In my area, we have Wegman's, who continues to grow their natural products selection to include vitamins and supplements as well as produce and packaged foods. A few years ago, they even beat out Whole Foods Market for best produce. Most restaurants now have vegetarian sections on their menu and are willing to make deviations from their menu to accommodate a client's needs. Because of this, it's now easier than ever to stick to your diet and avoid foods you've eliminated by asking the restaurant to tailor your order to your needs. Most restaurants are more than willing to accommodate you because they don't want you to get sick. They want you to be happy and give them good press.

When I was growing up, my mom made everything from scratch. We had a big garden, and we would freeze and can our fruits and vegetables to carry us through the winter. That was back when most people had gardens and there were farm stands on every corner. Now, with things like land development and both parents working out of the house in the corporate world, with kids having more homework and activities than ever before, preparing food seems to be the last thing on everyone's minds. Thankfully, we now have Farmer's Markets, CSAs, Door to Door Organics, and even Fresh Direct and other options, so that fresh, healthy food is readily available.

TRANSITIONING TO A VEGAN DIET

For me, the best way to transition from my former Standard American Diet (SAD) to my healthy lifestyle was to throw out all the foods that I was allergic to, or else give them away (there are a lot of food banks and needy people who could use the food). By cleaning out any foods that are no longer going to be a part of your life, you remove the temptation to go backwards. Remember, we always want to go forward in our life's journey.

Each time I grew in my journey, tweaking my diet/lifestyle as I went, I had to give up more foods and habits, as well as remove toxic people from my life. It's an unfortunate fact that some of your friends may not embrace your choice to live a healthy lifestyle. Stay strong; you can do it! Just remember that at the end of the day, you're the only one who has to live in your body.

When transitioning into a new diet and lifestyle, it's best to start off slow with small, manageable goals. Make just one change—like making a healthy smoothie for breakfast or lunch—and do that for a month. Don't overwhelm yourself; as long as you're moving forward, then the pace isn't as important.

Then, go through the list of recipes included in this book and try out any one of the lunch or dinner recipes that sound good to you. Keep expanding your palate and replacing your old meal standbys with healthy vegan alternatives, one by one, until you're completed your changeover. When I first changed my diet, it was easier for me to stick with just a couple of dishes, as that was easier for my body (and my overwhelmed brain) to handle!

By focusing on taking steps forward without looking back, you set yourself on the path to success by positioning your transition as a new adventure, rather than the sacrifice of your old lifestyle. Not to mention you'll start feeling better!

Keep in mind that you may experience a period of time where you actually feel like you have a cold. This is what's known as "die off." Now that you've started eating and living healthier, your body has started removing the toxins remaining in your body.

Personally, I got colonics during this time to help get rid of the die off more quickly. I also started taking digestive enzymes and probiotics during this time, and continue to do so today, as it helps to improve my digestion and the health of my gut. If you are not comfortable with colonics, your only option is to persevere. Take things easy for a while; be gentle with yourself and know that the die off *will* pass. Once it does, the change in your day-to-day energy levels and feelings of wellness will be like night and day.

ORGANIZING/PREPARING FOR YOUR VEGAN CHALLENGE

Organizing and preparing for your Vegan Challenge isn't any different than, say, painting a wall. When you paint a wall, you first prepare the room—taping up the woodwork, purchasing the paint, laying out your brushes, etc. When starting your Vegan Challenge, first make a list of the ingredients you will need to make each of your recipes. Make sure you have the appropriate equipment: for example, a blender or a food processor. Check how much time you need to make the dish, making sure not to set yourself up for frustration and failure. If you only have ten minutes to whip something together, then pick a simple smoothie recipe rather than an elaborate dish that takes an hour to prepare. My mom used to say, "Your eyes are bigger than your stomach!" Well, not much has changed, and I'm still guilty of buying the ingredients for three different recipes while only having time to make one.

On that note, if you're pressed for time, try to prioritize those recipes which are the most versatile. For example, my Three Nut Basil Pesto Pasta is a great recipe, and one where you can make the central element—the pesto—and use it for the recipe itself, or you can just spread it on crackers or use it stuff celery sticks. (It also makes a great filler for wraps, whether that be a collard or lettuce leaf or a Nori sheet.) See how you can take one recipe and extrapolate it to use it in numerous ways? It keeps things simple but interesting—and that includes your grocery list! I also make extra pesto and freeze it so that when I don't have time, I can just thaw out what I have already made. I also take it on vacation with me!

THE 30-DAY
VEGAN CHALLENGE

VEGAN CHALLENGE: DAY #1

Recipes
Breakfast: Creamsicle Morning

Lunch: Grilled Cheese

Dinner: Baked Sweet Potatoes

Daily Fact

For those of you who just can't live without your coffee, there is a caffeine-free herbal coffee alternative—Teeccino. Not being a coffee drinker myself, giving it up was never an issue for me, but for the many who are addicted to coffee, this can be a blessing. After I learned about Teeccino at the Institute of Integrative Nutrition, I shared it with one of my long-time coffee-drinking friends. She fell in love with it, immediately buying an assortment pack. Try it and see!

Daily Affirmation

"Life begins at the end of your comfort zone."

—NEALE DONALD WALSH

Challenger Notes / Log Entries

_____

_____

_____

_____

_____

_____

_____

VEGAN CHALLENGE: DAY #2

Recipes

Breakfast: Wheatgrass & Lemon Juice

Lunch: Vegan Quesadillas

Dinner: Collard Wrap

Daily Fact

I always start my day with juicing wheatgrass. Beginners should start by juicing one ounce per day, and you'll want to juice wheatgrass on an empty stomach. Do not gulp and/or chug your wheatgrass, as it is strong in flavor and very potent. I sip my wheatgrass and will usually swish it around in my mouth for a while before swallowing.

Daily Affirmation

"Don't try so hard to fit in when you were born to stand out!"

—ANONYMOUS

Challenger Notes / Log Entries

_____
_____
_____
_____
_____
_____
_____
_____
_____
_____

VEGAN CHALLENGE: DAY #3

Recipes

Breakfast: Lisa's Every Day Green Drink

Lunch: Quinoa Enchilada Casserole

Dinner: Heaven Soup

Daily Fact

What's great about Tribest is they have a family of juicers (and other healthy products) to meet your needs, whether it be your lifestyle, kitchen counter availability, or price point. I preach about Tribest products, not because I am an employee of Tribest (I'm not) but because I have been using their products for over ten years with no complaints. I have used my juicer consistently during that time, and it has held up well. I am sharing with you what has worked for me so you don't have to waste time searching.

Daily Affirmation

"The Greatest Glory in Living lies not in never falling. But in rising every time we fall."

—NELSON MANDELA, Greater Good Project

Challenger Notes / Log Entries

_____

_____

_____

_____

_____

_____

_____

VEGAN CHALLENGE: DAY #4

Recipes
Breakfast: Granola Fresh Fruit Parfait and Cashew Crème

Lunch: Baked Quinoa

Dinner: Corn Chowder

Daily Fact
Larabars: The basic ingredients in these raw/vegan bars are fruits, dates, and nuts. My favorite is the cashew flavored bar, which just contains cashews and dates. I keep them in the freezer for when I want a sweet treat or I am feeling just little bit hungry. It makes me feel like I'm eating a frozen Milky Way bar, just like I used to do as a child!

Daily Affirmation
"When one door closes another door opens. But we so often look so long and regretfully upon the closed door that we do not see the one that opens for us."

—ALEXANDER GRAHAM BELL

Challenger Notes / Log Entries

VEGAN CHALLENGE: DAY #5

Recipes
Breakfast: Pomaberry Slushee

Lunch: Quinoa Tabbouleh

Dinner: Creamy Carob Mousse

Daily Fact
Awesome Foods not only makes an assortment of fresh vegan raw foods to go, like hummus, pizza, lasagna, un-tuna salad, and an assortment of other salads, but they also have a whole line of dry products, such as raw crackers, raw bars, and tempura-covered veggies, to name a few. They are prepackaged and are the perfect size to throw in your suitcase or lunch box.

Daily Affirmation
"Contentment is not the fulfillment of what we want but the realization of how much you have."

—KIKI KNICKERBOCKER

Challenger Notes / Log Entries

_____

_____

_____

_____

_____

_____

_____

_____

VEGAN CHALLENGE: DAY #6

Recipes
Breakfast: Strawberry Choco-Nanna Smoothie

Lunch: Vegan Thai Curry

Dinner: Zucchini, Carrot, and Cucumber Salad

Daily Fact
Go Raw has an assortment of pre-made raw crackers, bars, and cookies that are packaged ready-to-eat and to-go. They are a perfect size to throw in your lunchbox, tote bag, or suitcase. I used to spend hours making my own crackers, but when you have limited time, I've found it's so much easier to buy a small bag of healthy crackers that are packaged airtight, meaning they won't go stale before you have a chance to use them.

Daily Affirmation
"You gain strength, courage, and confidence by every experience in which you really stop to look fear in the face. You must do the thing you think you cannot do."

—Eleanor Roosevelt

Challenger Notes / Log Entries

_____

_____

_____

_____

_____

_____

VEGAN CHALLENGE: DAY #7

Recipes
Breakfast: Morning Pick Me Up
Lunch: Grilled Tasty Vegetables
Dinner: Healthy Minestrone Soup

Daily Fact
When I'm traveling by airplane, I obviously can't take my juicer and wheat-grass with me. So I asked my acupuncturist, who is a walking encyclopedia on truly healthy living, about what brand of powdered wheatgrass he recommends. He recommended Amazing Grass Organic Powdered Wheat-grass, which can be purchased on Amazon or at your local healthy market like Kimberton Whole Foods (and even some progressive mainstream markets). Amazing Grass is gluten-free, no sugar added, and plant-based. If you aren't into juicing or don't have the time, space, and finances, this is a good alternative.

Daily Affirmation
"While we may not be able to control all that happens to us, we can control what happens inside us."

—BEN FRANKLIN

Challenger Notes / Log Entries

_____

_____

_____

_____

_____

_____

VEGAN CHALLENGE: DAY #8

Recipes

Breakfast: Tropical Snow Smoothie

Lunch: Oven-Roasted Butternut Squash

Dinner: Spiced Kuri Squash Soup

Daily Fact

Daiya not only has vegan cheeses and sour cream, but also provide frozen gluten-free pizzas with vegan cheese that you can throw in the oven, bake, and eat. Macaroni and cheese, an established comfort food for most people, is provided by Daiya with their line of Cheezy Mac options. Daiya also has salad dressings, Greek yogurt, and cheese cake, all dairy-free and vegan.

Daily Affirmation

"Yesterday I wanted to change the world. Today I want to change myself."

—RUMI

Challenger Notes / Log Entries

_____

_____

_____

_____

_____

_____

_____

_____

VEGAN CHALLENGE: DAY #9

Recipes
Breakfast: Strawberry-Mango Coulis

Lunch: Ratatouille

Dinner: Seaweed and Shitake Salad

Daily Fact
Wheatgrass is the true superfood. Here are just a few of its many benefits:
- Contains more sunlight energy than any other food
- Restores fertility and promotes youthfulness
- Assists in sugar leveling
- Works as a purifier, cleanser, and detoxifier, and removes heavy metals from the body
- Arrests the growth of unfriendly bacteria

Daily Affirmation
"Hope begins in the dark when you look out at the light."

—FROM HALLMARK'S *THE CHRISTMAS TRAIN*

Challenger Notes / Log Entries

_____

_____

_____

_____

_____

_____

_____

_____

VEGAN CHALLENGE: DAY #10

Recipes
Breakfast: Vanilla Crème Smoothie

Lunch: Cooked Wild Rice and Chickpea Salad

Dinner: Superfood Kale Avocado Salad with Raw Olives

Daily Fact
Just Veggn' provides a premade frozen vegetable patty that you can bake or stir-fry. You can serve it as a basic burger, cut it in small pieces and add it to your salad, or eat it as an appetizer. Angie Ritter of Just Veggn' has shared several recipes in this book to give you some ideas on how to use her burgers.

Daily Affirmation
"It's not how much we give, but how much love we put into giving."

—MOTHER TERESA

Challenger Notes / Log Entries

_____

_____

_____

_____

_____

_____

_____

_____

_____

_____

VEGAN CHALLENGE: DAY #11

Recipes
Breakfast: Carrot Beet Celery Juice

Lunch: Mediterranean Layer Pie

Dinner: Happy Harvest Salad

Daily Fact
Explore Asia has vegan, kosher, and gluten-free pasta that comes in spaghetti and fettucine shapes. For those of you who don't want to spiralize fresh vegetables, this is the next best thing. Cooking directions are provided on the package, and they're as easy to use as they are to eat.

Daily Affirmation
"The noblest art is that of making others happy."

—P. T. Barnum

Challenger Notes / Log Entries

_____

_____

_____

_____

_____

_____

_____

_____

_____

_____

_____

VEGAN CHALLENGE: DAY #12

Recipes

Breakfast: Blueberry Grape Smoothie

Lunch: Quick Quinoa with Cilantro Pesto

Dinner: Sautéed Brussel Sprouts

Daily Fact

Harmless Harvest is still my favorite coconut water. Not everyone is up to cracking open their own coconuts to clean out the coconut meat or water. Plus, it's much easier to carry a bottle of Harmless Harvest Coconut Water to the gym than to bring along a young Thai coconut.

Daily Affirmation

"The cave you fear to enter holds the treasure that you seek."

—JOSEPH CAMPBELL

Challenger Notes / Log Entries

_____

_____

_____

_____

_____

_____

_____

_____

_____

_____

VEGAN CHALLENGE: DAY #13

Recipes
Breakfast: Watermelon-Strawberry Thirst Quencher
Lunch: Patty Up® with Beans, Rice and Veggies
Dinner: Raw Cashew Cheese

Daily Fact
Treeline nut cheese is a cheese made from raw cashews, probiotics, and seasonings. Treeline has a creamy, soft French-style cheese that comes in a tub with several different flavors (my favorites are the herb-garlic and scallion). They also have a hard classic aged cheese in regular and cracked pepper. They taste like real cheese but with only healthy ingredients and no chemicals. It is non-dairy, contains no cholesterol, is non-GMO, gluten-free, probiotic, and contains no soy or lactose.

Daily Affirmation
"Every day is a second chance."
—FROM HALLMARK'S *WITH LOVE, CHRISTMAS*

Challenger Notes / Log Entries

_____

_____

_____

_____

_____

_____

_____

VEGAN CHALLENGE: DAY #14

Recipes

Breakfast: Basic Almond Milk

Lunch: Sautéed Hiziki with Spring Vegetables

Dinner: Baked Avocado with Cherry Tomatoes

Daily Fact

A study done by Nobel Prize winner Elizabeth Blackburn found that a vegan diet caused more than 500 genes to change in three months, turning on genes that prevent disease and turning off genes that cause cancer, heart disease, and other illnesses.

Daily Affirmation

"Sometimes broken roads lead to the best destiny."

—FROM HALLMARK'S *THE CHRISTMAS PARADE*

Challenger Notes / Log Entries

VEGAN CHALLENGE: DAY #15

Recipes
Breakfast: Fresh Orange Juice

Lunch: Marinated Lotus Roots

Dinner: Lentil Vegetable Soup

Daily Fact
Eating one to two servings of salad with spinach, lettuce, and kale daily may keep your brain eleven years younger, as well as prevent dementia, according to a study performed by the Rush University in Chicago.

Daily Affirmation
"Life is messy. When we get thru the mess, we find out who we really are."

FROM HALLMARK'S *WITH LOVE, CHRISTMAS*

Challenger Notes / Log Entries

_____

_____

_____

_____

_____

_____

_____

_____

_____

_____

_____

_____

VEGAN CHALLENGE: DAY #16

Recipes
Breakfast: Pineapple Smoothie

Lunch: Eggplant Bacon

Dinner: Quinoa Porridge with Grilled Zucchini

Daily Fact
The Black Dog Institute in Sydney, Australia, determined that even one hour of exercise a week can help prevent depression.

Daily Affirmation
"Memories build the bridge between our mind and heart."

—From Hallmark's *Magical Christmas Ornaments*

Challenger Notes / Log Entries

_____

_____

_____

_____

_____

_____

_____

_____

_____

_____

_____

_____

VEGAN CHALLENGE: DAY #17

Recipes
Breakfast: FROG (Fig-Raspberry-Orange-Ginger) Smoothie
Lunch: Steamed Cruciferous Vegetables with Tangy Tahini Dressing
Dinner: Mung Bean Stew

Daily Fact
Finding you can't focus? Ten minutes of exercise gives the brain a burst of energy to help you focus and stay on task, according to a study performed by Western University in London, Ontario.

Daily Affirmation
"If God gives us a dream, he will give us the ability to achieve it."

—ANONYMOUS

Challenger Notes / Log Entries

_____

_____

_____

_____

_____

_____

_____

_____

_____

_____

_____

VEGAN CHALLENGE: DAY #18

Recipes
Breakfast: Green Supreme Smoothie

Lunch: Spaghetti Squash and Greens

Dinner: Creamy Carrot Soup with Potato

Daily Fact
Personally, I run my wheatgrass through my Tribest Greenstar Elite Juicer. I had heard about the Tribest's Greenstar Juicer for several years before I finally got my first model, and it was so worth the wait. After using other juicers that forced me to do things like run the pulp through multiple times to get the end result I wanted, the Greenstar Elite saved me both time and aggravation.

Daily Affirmation
"A man travels the world over in search of what he needs, and returns home and finds it."

—GEORGE A. MOORE

Challenger Notes / Log Entries

_____

_____

_____

_____

_____

_____

_____

_____

VEGAN CHALLENGE: DAY #19

Recipes
Breakfast: Pineapple Apple Sunset Juice

Lunch: Roasted Vegetables

Dinner: Alkaline Umeboshi

Daily Fact
Studies have linked leaving the house and staying active to increased longevity and improved energy levels in older adults. So don't just stay in, get out there!

Daily Affirmation
"If your actions inspire others to
  …dream more
  …learn more
  …do more…then you are a leader."

—President John Quincy Adams

Challenger Notes / Log Entries

_____

_____

_____

_____

_____

_____

_____

_____

_____

VEGAN CHALLENGE: DAY #20

Recipes
Breakfast: Chai Nut Milk

Lunch: Walnut Fiesta Burrito

Dinner: 3 Mushroom Medley

Daily Fact

In 1997, research teams at John Hopkins concluded that broccoli sprouts promote more cancer protection and antioxidant activity than broccoli alone, thanks to a unique compound called sulforaphane. (Now you know why I started adding broccoli sprouts to my smoothies!)

Daily Affirmation

"Believe in yourself and all that you are. Know that there is something inside you that is greater than any obstacle."

—CHRISTIAN D. LARSON

Challenger Notes / Log Entries

_____

_____

_____

_____

_____

_____

_____

_____

_____

_____

VEGAN CHALLENGE: DAY #21

Recipes
Breakfast: Start the Day Smoothie

Lunch: Warm Zucchini Noodle Red Pepper Spice Roast

Dinner: Shallot-Pistachio-Balsamic Brussels Sprouts

Daily Fact
Dandy Blend is an instant herbal beverage made with dandelions that serves as a coffee alternative. Great both cold and hot, it's a great way to get dandelion in your diet. I use it in the summer over ice as my alternative to iced tea. The ingredients are extracts of roasted barley, rye, chicory root, dandelion, and sugar beet, with no GMOs. It's also gluten free, 100 percent caffeine-free, and has no acidity or bitterness.

Daily Affirmation
"You are the message."

—ROGER AILES

Challenger Notes / Log Entries

_____

_____

_____

_____

_____

_____

_____

_____

_____

VEGAN CHALLENGE: DAY #22

Recipes
Breakfast: Strawberry Apple Juice

Lunch: Vegan-Style Patty Up®

Dinner: Build Your Own Vegan Bowl

Daily Fact
Sherrie Burrell of Burris Consulting created "Patty Up," a vegan or vegetarian "patty" mixture (depending on what you add to the mixture). The mixture is gluten-free, non-GMO, no soy, low sodium, and does not contain preservatives. In addition to making burgers with the mixture, you can create chili, meatballs, and meatloaf. Sherrie has graciously shared some of her recipes with us in this collection to get you started.

Daily Affirmation
"The only thing necessary for triumph of evil is for good people to do nothing."

—EDMUND BURKE

Challenger Notes / Log Entries

_____

_____

_____

_____

_____

_____

_____

_____

VEGAN CHALLENGE: DAY #23

Recipes

Breakfast: Demo Delight Smoothie

Lunch: Twelve Superfoods Salad

Dinner: Smokey Mushroom Risotto

Daily Fact

Quinoa has been around for thousands of years. Native Andean populations have long cultivated the grain, as its high iron content makes it perfect for people living in high-altitude, oxygen-poor areas like the Andes.

Daily Affirmation

"It's not enough to just show up. You must participate. If not you...who?"

—ANNE ANSTINE, Professor of Women's Leadership

Challenger Notes / Log Entries

_____

_____

_____

_____

_____

_____

_____

_____

_____

_____

_____

_____

VEGAN CHALLENGE: DAY #24

Recipes
Breakfast: Apple Carrot Juice

Lunch: Family Potato Pancakes

Dinner: Cauliflower Stir Fry with Tofu

Daily Fact
Drinking alkaline water—water with a lower acidity than tap water—can reduce incidence of acid reflux, as well as improve overall energy levels and metabolism thanks to its antioxidant properties.

Daily Affirmation
JUST FOR TODAY: I will live through THIS DAY ONLY. I will not brood about yesterday or obsess about tomorrow. I will not set far-reaching goals or try to overcome all of my problems at once.

    I know that I can do something for twenty-four hours that would overwhelm me if I had to keep it up for a lifetime.

Challenger Notes / Log Entries

_____

_____

_____

_____

_____

_____

_____

_____

VEGAN CHALLENGE: DAY #25

Recipes

Breakfast: Wheatgrass/Apple

Lunch: Chocolate Berry Avocado Smoothie Bowl

Dinner: Very Basic Hummus

Daily Fact

More benefits of wheatgrass include:

- Contains 50+ minerals and vitamins (which is why I called wheatgrass "liquid gold"). Two ounces of juiced wheatgrass is equivalent to 5.5 pounds of leafy greens!
- Increases and strengthens red blood cell count, lowers blood pressure, and restores alkalinity to the blood.
- Stimulates the thyroid gland, helping with obesity and indigestion.
- Helps treat peptic ulcers, ulcerative colitis, constipation, and diarrhea.

Daily Affirmation

JUST FOR TODAY: I will be happy. I will not dwell on thoughts that depress me. If my mind fills with clouds, I will chase them away and fill it with sunshine.

Challenger Notes / Log Entries

VEGAN CHALLENGE: DAY #26

Recipes
Breakfast: Pumpkin Spice & Everything Nice Smoothie

Lunch: Hot Artichoke Dip

Dinner: Coco Nori Raw Savory Wrap

Daily Fact
Coconut Wraps is another all-natural alternative to bread and tortillas. It's raw, vegan, gluten-free, non-GMO, and kosher. You can fill this with your favorite ingredients, then roll, wrap, and eat. I also like the coconut wraps as a dessert wrap. You can fill it with fresh fruit and cashew crème (see page 52 for my recipe!)

Daily Affirmation
JUST FOR TODAY: I will accept what is. I will face reality. I will correct those things that I can correct and accept those I cannot.

Challenger Notes / Log Entries

_____

_____

_____

_____

_____

_____

_____

_____

_____

_____

_____

VEGAN CHALLENGE: DAY #27

Recipes
Breakfast: Another One of Lisa's Favorite Green Juices
Lunch: Pesto Vegetables
Dinner: Gandules Con Coco (Green Pigeon Peas with Coconut)

Daily Fact
Even more benefits of wheatgrass!
- Detoxifies the liver and protectors blood in the bloodstream
- Assists in fighting tumors and neutralizes toxins
- Stimulates a rapid cleaning of the colon and promotes regular bowel movement
- Makes a great antiseptic for cuts, burns, scrapes, and rashes

Daily Affirmation
JUST FOR TODAY: I will improve my mind. I will read something that requires effort, thought, and concentration. I will not be a mental loafer.

Challenger Notes / Log Entries

_____

_____

_____

_____

_____

_____

_____

_____

_____

VEGAN CHALLENGE: DAY #28

Recipes

Breakfast: Un-Egg Nog

Lunch: GBG'S (Grains, Beans and Greens)

Dinner: Roasted Red Pepper and Asparagus

Daily Fact

Have you helped someone today? Given someone a smile, held open a door, offered a kind word? Even the smallest acts of kindness ripple outwards, making the world around you a better place.

Daily Affirmation

JUST FOR TODAY: I will make a conscious effort to be agreeable. I will be kind and courteous to those who cross my path, and I'll not speak ill of others, I will improve my appearance, speak softly, and not interrupt when someone else is talking. Just for today, I will refrain from improving anybody but myself.

Challenger Notes / Log Entries

_____

_____

_____

_____

_____

_____

_____

_____

VEGAN CHALLENGE: DAY #29

Recipes
Breakfast: Pina Colada Green Smoothie

Lunch: Shirley's Patty Up® Vegetarian Meat Balls with Sweet Red Sauce

Dinner: Broccoli Salad with Tahini Sauce

Daily Fact
Parsley contains strong antioxidants which strengthen the body's immune system.

Daily Affirmation
JUST FOR TODAY: I will do something positive to improve my health. If I'm a smoker, I'll quit. If I am overweight, I will eat healthfully--if only just for today. And not only that, I will get off the couch and take a brisk walk, even if it's only around the block.

Challenger Notes / Log Entries

_____

_____

_____

_____

_____

_____

_____

_____

_____

_____

VEGAN CHALLENGE: DAY #30

Recipes
Breakfast: Carrot Apple Ginger Juice

Lunch: Raw Traditional Pizza

Dinner: Spicy Vegan Wraps with Tangy Almond Sauce

Daily Fact
I met the founders of WrawP a few years ago at the Natural Products Show East and fell in love with their products. Their wraps are clean, vegan, gluten-free, and raw. They're also incredibly easy to use; you can just fill them up with your favorite filler and you are good to go. I like that the people from WrawP have made a great product that is healthy and tastes good. Plus, I love the co-owners, Elizabeth (founder) and Kraig.

Daily Affirmation
JUST FOR TODAY: I will gather the courage to do what is right and take responsibility for my own actions.

Challenger Notes / Log Entries

_____

_____

_____

_____

_____

_____

_____

_____

THE RECIPES

People always ask me what I eat for breakfast, especially since so many people skip breakfast or just grab a cup of coffee on their way to work. Everyone's always in a rush; they don't realize how important breakfast is to your body. You are literally "breaking your fast" from when you were sleeping; our bodies need breakfast to provide fuel to get our engines going.

When I was a little girl, I remember my mom reading in a lady's magazine that we should eat a king-sized breakfast, a queen-sized lunch, and a pauper-sized dinner. Today, people tend to have it backwards, eating their big meal of the day at dinner, only to wonder why they can't sleep. By now, I'm sure you've heard that you should eat no less than three hours before you go to bed if you want to lose weight. Ironically, since I started working in corporate America forty years ago, my big meal of the day after breakfast is lunch. After work I'll exercise, and by the time I get home from the gym, the last thing I want to do is prepare a meal. Even when I go out with friends, I always try to steer our meal outings towards lunch time. I have found that when I eat a large dinner, I'm up all night as my body tries to digest the food.

My friends and I are going to share some of our favorite healthy breakfast recipes, the ones that work best for us. Whether you use these as-is or as a guide for your own creations, these recipes are intended to give you the ultimate start to your day. Remember: the start of your day is going to set the tone for the next twenty-four hours. Don't beat yourself up if transforming your life takes time, trial, and error. We are all works in progress!

Start the Day Smoothie

Prep Time: 10 minutes

1 tray ice cubes

1 scoop chocolate Raw Organic Fit Vegetarian Protein Powder by Garden of Life

1 tablespoon raw cacao

1 tablespoon maca

⅛ teaspoon Shilajit powder

1 teaspoon Organic Mushroom Lion's Mane powder

2 bananas

1 fluid ounce Liquid Colloidal Minerals

4 dandelion leaves

¼ cup broccoli sprouts

⅓ cup organic blueberries (frozen)

2–3 cups almond milk

1 tablespoon raw cacao nibs

Combine all the ingredients (except the raw cacao nibs) in a high-speed blender. Pour smoothie into a glass and sprinkle the raw cacao nibs on top.

Lisa's Note: *After I drink my wheatgrass, I like to follow it with my "Start-The-Day Smoothie." I've been making this smoothie for a good two or three years, and I still haven't gotten tired of it!*

Basic Almond Milk

Prep: 10 minutes

2 cups raw soaked almonds
9–12 dates, pitted
1–2 tablespoon alcohol-free vanilla flavoring
6 cups water

Combine ingredients in a high-speed blender and blend on high until thoroughly blended. Place a nut milk bag in a large bowl and pour the mixture through the bag. Milk the milk bag (like you are milking a cow) until all the milk comes out.

Lisa's Note: *I like to store my almond milk in Ball jars in my refrigerator. Screw the lid on securely to make sure it doesn't spill. You can also freeze the pulp and save it for later to make crackers, croutons, or almond pulp pate.*

Wheatgrass

Prep: 5 minutes

Wheatgrass

Run wheatgrass through your Tribest Greenstar Elite Juicer. Beginners should start by juicing 1 ounce per day.

> **Lisa's Note:** *Wheatgrass is known for its healing and detoxifying properties. When you drink wheatgrass, it's best to sip the juice slowly and swish it around in your mouth for a while before swallowing. Do not chug your wheatgrass quickly, as it is very strong; if you drink it too quickly, it can upset your stomach. It's also best to drink your wheatgrass on an empty stomach, which is why I start my day with wheat grass juice. Wheatgrass has more than fifty vitamins and minerals—that's why I call it liquid gold!.*

Lisa's Every Day Green Drink

Prep: 7 minutes

½ to 1 lemon, cut to fit juicer
1 cucumber, cut into spears to fit juicer
4 celery stalks
6 apples, cut into wedges to fit juicer
Handful of your favorite greens

Feed all ingredients into a Tribest Greenstar Elite Juicer. Stir and drink.

Note: You can adjust the above ingredients to taste, or even toss in some additional vegetables such as carrots, ginger, parsley, cabbage, or beets—whatever you have on hand will be fine.

Wheatgrass & Lemon Juice

Prep: 5 minutes

2 ounces wheatgrass
Spritz of lemon juice

Run wheatgrass through your Tribest Greenstar Elite juicer. You can either run a wedge of lemon through the juicer or cut a lemon wedge and squeeze it by hand in to your wheatgrass. Stir and drink (by swishing). People who don't like the taste of wheatgrass by itself often find it enjoyable after adding some lemon, so give it a try!

Granola Fresh Fruit Parfait and Cashew Crème

Prep: 45 minutes

Granola
2 cups buckwheat groats,
    soaked overnight
1 cup raw almonds, soaked
2 apples, cored and
    chopped fine
½ cup shredded coconut
    (optional)
½ cup raisins, dried
    cranberries, or dried
    blueberries
¼ cup goji berries
½ cup soaked flaxseeds
1 teaspoon cinnamon
1 cup dates, pitted
2 bananas, pureed
1 tablespoon vanilla
Pinch sea salt

Cashew Crème
1 cup raw cashews, soaked
    and drained
1 tablespoon agave
1 tablespoon vanilla
Water, as needed

Fresh Fruit Parfait
1 sliced banana
Fresh berries of your
    choice (blueberries,
    strawberries, and
    raspberries)
1 apple, sliced, cored, and
    cut into bite-size pieces
Fresh squeezed orange
    juice
Raw cacao nibs for garnish
    (optional)
Raw almond slivers for
    garnish (optional)

Granola
Combine ingredients in a food processor, then spread out on a Teflex-lined dehydrator sheet and dehydrate at 105ºF until doneness desired. Remember to flip halfway through.

Cashew Crème

In a high-speed blender, blend the cashews, agave, and vanilla, adding enough water so the mixture blends into a crème. Don't add too much water; you want this to be a crème, and not runny.

Fresh Fruit Parfait

Take a Ball jar or parfait dish and start layering fruit, followed by granola, followed by cashew crème. Pour in fresh orange juice and top with a few slivers of raw almonds and raw cacao nibs. You can also make dish in a bowl instead of ball jar or parfait dish.

Watermelon Juice

Prep: 5 minutes

Watermelon meat, removed from rind

Cut watermelon meat from rind and blend together in a Vitamix high-speed blender.

> **Lisa's Note:** *By now, everyone knows I adore watermelon juice. I love to drink it after exercising. It quenches my thirst, it's cool and refreshing, and if you have a sweet tooth, a glass of watermelon juice will take care of the sweet cravings.*
>
> *It's also great for hydration, aids in weight loss, and serves as an anti-inflammatory and a diuretic, as well as being alkaline-forming. Drink watermelon juice slowly and on an empty stomach. Always wait thirty minutes after you drink or eat watermelon before you eat anything else.*

Wheatgrass/Apple

Prep: 5 minutes

8 ounces apple juice
2 ounces wheatgrass

Run apple juice and wheatgrass through your Greenstar Elite Juicer. Stir and drink (by swishing).

Pomaberry Slushee

Olivia de Maigret

Prep: 7–10 minutes
Serves: 2

1 cup fresh pomegranate juice
1 cup mixed berries (fresh or frozen)
1 tablespoon raw agave nectar
2 teaspoons fresh squeezed lemon juice
10 ice cubes
½ cup distilled water
2 sprigs fresh mint

Place all ingredients except mint in a high-speed blender. Blend for about 1 minute, or until the mixture becomes smooth with the texture of a slush drink. Be careful not to over-blend, as the mixture will become too watery. Serve immediately in a tall clear glass. Garnish with mint leaves and enjoy!

Lisa's Note: *What makes this recipe and its creator Olivia de Maigret so special is that she was only eleven years old when she created the recipe. Olivia, her mom Kathryn, and I had the pleasure of vacationing in Bali during October of 2014. We were there at the same time, staying in the same hotel, and even had the same tour guide. We all became instant friends, and we plan on staying connected forever.*

Olivia created this recipe all by herself without anyone's help. I've heard people saying, "Oh, I can't eat healthy," or, "It's too hard," or, "I can't come up with recipes." But if Olivia can create this amazing recipe at the young age of eleven, you too can eat healthy and create recipes—no matter what your age.

Note that if you are using store bought pomegranate juice, buy varieties that have no sugar added (Olivia prefers the POM brand).

Strawberry Apple Juice

Prep: 7 minutes

¼ cup strawberries
2 apples, cored

Slice apples so that they can fit through the feeder of the juicer.
Feed apples and strawberries through the feeder of the Tribest
Greenstar Elite Juicer. Stir and drink.

Apple Carrot Juice

Prep: 8 minutes

2 apples, cored
6 carrots

Slice apples and carrots so they can be fed through the juicer. I do not peel the apples or carrots, as I prefer to use organic vegetables. Feed through juicer. Stir and drink.

Lisa's Note: *Carrots and apples help with digestion, as well as help minerals to be absorbed into your system. My Aunt Elsie used to juice carrot juice for my Uncle Joe daily when I was a little girl, and he lived well into his nineties!*

Carrot Apple Ginger Juice

Prep: 7 minutes

1 cup carrots
1 cup apples
1 sliver ginger

Slice ingredients to fit through the feed section of the Tribest Elite Juicer. You do not need to remove the seeds, stem, or skin of the apple. All parts of the apple will be juiced. Feed the ingredients through the juicer. Stir and drink. Note that you can change the ingredient portions of this recipe based upon whether you like more carrot then apple, or vice versa. Use what you have and use the ingredients you like.

Carrot Beet Celery Juice

Prep: 10 minutes

1 cup carrots
1 cup beets
1 large stalk celery

Cut the beets to fit in to the Tribest Greenstar Elite Juicer (no need to peel the beets). As you may have learned by now, in many cases, the skin is the most nutritious part of the fruit and/or vegetable. Run the carrots, beets, and celery through the juicer. Stir, drink, enjoy, and feel energized. Feel free to switch up the proportions to your liking.

Pineapple Apple Sunset Juice

Prep: 10 minutes

1 (1-inch) slice pineapple

2 large apples

1 teaspoon mint

⅛ cup parsley

¼ cup greens (lettuce, spinach, kale, etc.)

Slice the ingredients to fit through the feeding tube of the Tribest Greenstar Elite Juicer. Run ingredients through the juicer and juice. Stir and drink.

Creamsicle Morning

Prep: 5 minutes

1–2 oranges, peeled
1–2 cups almond milk
2–3 bananas, peeled
1 tablespoon alcohol-free vanilla
1 tray ice cubes

Combine ingredients in a high-speed blender and serve.

Vanilla Crème Smoothie

Prep: 7 minutes

2 tablespoon alcohol-free vanilla
1 tablespoon Singing Dog vanilla, alcohol free
9 dates, pitted
16 ounces raw almond milk
1 tray ice

Combine ingredients in a high-speed blender until desired consistency is reached. You can also add extra ingredients to help support your health and well-being, such as liquid aloe vera, Shilajit, or trace minerals. If a tray of ice is too chilling for you, try freezing your bananas and add water to equal the amount of one tray of ice.

Pumpkin Spice & Everything Nice Smoothie

Prep: 7 minutes

3 bananas, peeled

4 ounces fruit, pumpkin, or butternut squash (peeled if
     pumpkin or squash)

1 medjool date

1 tray ice cubes

8–12 ounces raw almond milk

½–1 teaspoon pumpkin spice or to taste

Combine ingredients in a high-speed blender and blend until desired consistency is reached. Pumpkin Spice typically includes cinnamon, ginger, clove, and nutmeg. If you don't have pumpkin spice at home, you can use these individual spices or come up with your own blend. Experiment; feel free to become a mad scientist in your kitchen!

Strawberry Orange Smoothie

Prep: 5 minutes

4–6 ounces fresh or frozen strawberries (with stems and leaves)
2 oranges (peeled and quartered)
Handful of greens
3 bananas
1 tray of ice cubes
Water (to cover ingredients)
1 medjool date
Sprig of fresh mint (optional)

Place all ingredients in a high-speed blender and blend until the mixture comes to a smooth consistency.

Blueberry Grape Smoothie

Prep: 5 minutes

½ cup frozen or fresh grapes
½ cup frozen or fresh blueberries
3 bananas, peeled
1 young Thai coconut (meat and juice)
1 tray ice cubes
1 medjool date

Combine ingredients together in a high-speed blender until smooth. If you don't have a high-speed blender, use whatever blender you have available.

Peach Orange Smoothie

Prep: 7 minutes

2 oranges, peeled
2–3 bananas, peeled
3 peaches, pitted
1 medjool date
1/3–½ cup water
1 tray ice cubes
Raw cacao nibs (optional)

Combine ingredients in a high-speed blender until smooth, hence the name smmooottthhhiiiee! Optionally, you can add raw cacao nibs sprinkles on top of the smoothie. Who said breakfast can't look good, taste good, feel good, *and* be good for you?

Lisa's Note: *Sometimes I'll use juice as the liquid part of my smoothie (mostly orange juice). The juices give the drink extra flavor, freshness, and lightness.*

THE RECIPES

Demo Delight Smoothie

Prep: 7 minutes

1 cup fresh strawberries

1 orange, peeled

2–3 bananas

1 medjool date

1–2 tablespoon raw cacao

1 tray ice

Water, enough for desired smoothness

Blend ingredients together in your high-speed blender.

Lisa's Note: *I usually make this smoothie for demos, primarily because I like myth-busting. People can't believe that you can actually have chocolate-flavored food and have it still be good for you. Just remember: raw chocolate is considered a super food. Healthy food can taste good, be easy to make, and still be good for you. This smoothie is loved by people young and old.*

Chai Nut Milk

Prep time: 15 minutes

1½ teaspoons garam marsala
1 teaspoon ground ginger
1 teaspoon cinnamon
½ teaspoon ground cardamom
½ teaspoon nutmeg

Add the above spices to your almond milk mixture when blending in your Vitamix® High Speed Blender. Store nut milk in a large canning jar with lid in your refrigerator. You will drink it up before it goes bad.

Coconut Milk and Coconut Water

Prep: 5 minutes

1 young Thai Coconut

Use the back end of a cleaver knife and cut a circle around the top of the coconut. To make coconut water, simply pour the liquid out from the young Thai coconut after opening and drink.

For coconut milk, blend the coconut water and the meat (which you can remove from the inside of the coconut using an ice cream scoop) together in a Vitamix high-speed blender.

Pineapple Smoothie

Prep time: 5 minutes

1½-inch thick slice of fresh pineapple
3 bananas
1 medjool date
1 tray ice cube
12 ounces almond milk

Blend ingredients together in a Vitamix® High Speed Blender until smooth.

Lisa's Green Smoothie

3 bananas
2 pears
1-inch-thick slice fresh pineapple
1 medjool date
3–4 leaves kale or assorted greens
1 young Thai coconut (meat and water)

Add all ingredients to a high-speed blender and blend until smooth. Pour into a glass and drink.

Strawberry Choco-Nanna Smoothie

3 fresh bananas
1 tray ice cubes
1 cup strawberries
1–2 heaping tablespoons raw cacao or carob powder
1 teaspoon agave syrup
2 cups almond milk

In a high-powered blender, blend all ingredients until creamy.
Pour into drinking glasses and enjoy.

Un-Egg Nog

Prep: 15 minutes

2 cups almond milk

3 fresh bananas

¼ teaspoon Sun Organics alcohol-free vanilla extract

¼ teaspoon cinnamon

Pinch sea salt

2–3 dates pitted

¼ teaspoon nutmeg, grated (to taste)

Place all the ingredients in a high-speed blender and blend until smooth. Add additional dates if you wish the nog to be sweeter. Serve immediately with a dash of grated nutmeg on top.

Watermelon-Strawberry Thirst Quencher

Prep: 15 minutes

3 cups watermelon
1 cup strawberries
1 lime, juiced
2 dates, pitted
1 tray ice cubes

Combine the above ingredients in a Vitamix® blender.

Fresh Orange Juice

4 medium oranges (approximately 8 ounces juiced)

Place oranges in a Tribest Citristar (or any juicer) and juice. Drink and enjoy.

Morning Pick Me Up

Prep: 15 minutes

4 carrots
2 apples
1 pear
2 oranges
1 lemon

Run the above ingredients together through your Tribest Green-Star juicer. Cool and refreshing!

Another One of Lisa's Favorite Green Juices

2 cucumbers
4 celery stalks
½–1 cup sunflower sprouts
3 pears
1 lemon (juice only)

Run all the ingredients through the juicer. Drink and enjoy.

Strawberry-Mango Coulis

Prep: 15 minutes

3 cups strawberries, hulled
1 cup mango, cubed
1 cup dates, pitted and packed
1 tablespoon lemon juice
½ tablespoon lime juice
Water (as needed)

Combine ingredients in a high speed-blender and use water as needed to blend well. Refrigerate in a glass jar with lid.

Tropical Snow Smoothie

1 mango or papaya
1 1-inch slice fresh pineapple
1 tray ice cubes
3 bananas
1 young Thai coconut (meat and juice)
Handful cacao nibs
1 medjool date

Combine all ingredients in a high-speed blender.

FROG (Fig-Raspberry-Orange-Ginger) Smoothie

3 figs, pitted
1½ cups raspberries
2 oranges, peeled and seeded
¼-inch piece ginger
3 bananas
1 young Thai coconut
1 tray ice cubes

Combine all of the ingredients together in a high-speed blender and enjoy.

Pina Colada Green Smoothie
Jenny Tolnay

Makes: 2 large smoothies

2 cups water or coconut water

3 cups spinach

1 green apple

1 kiwi

1 cup frozen broccoli

1 banana, frozen

1 cup mango chunks, frozen

1 cup pineapple chunks, frozen

1 cup strawberries, fresh or frozen

3 tablespoons coconut flakes

1 scoop hemp protein powder (optional)

1 tablespoon flax seed (optional)

1 teaspoon amla powder (optional)

Blend spinach and water in a high-speed blender. Add apple and kiwi and blend. Add frozen ingredients one at a time and blend (you may need to let frozen ingredients thaw a bit depending on how powerful your blender is). Add coconut flakes and optional add-ins and blend until smooth. Pour into glasses and serve.

Green Supreme Smoothie

Olivia de Maigret

Serves: 1–2

1 generous handful baby spinach
1 cup homemade (or store bought) almond milk
1 teaspoon raw cacao nibs
1 medjool date
½ cup fresh frozen blueberries
Half a banana
3 ice cubes

Combine all ingredients in a high-speed blender.

After breakfast, lunch is my biggest meal of the day. Something you'll find when you eat nutritionally dense food is that you end up eating a whole lot less. It doesn't take much to fill me up.

As a rule of thumb, you should eat when you are hungry, not just because it happens to be noon. Also, don't keep eating until you feel so stuffed that it hurts. Your parents were probably like mine and raised you to clean your plate, even if you were already full. I even use a lunch-size plate for my meals now, so I don't feel obliged to fill the plate and eat everything on the plate.

Even though I don't tend to eat dinner as such, I know many of you do, so I've also noted which recipes I think are better suited for lunch—usually heavier recipes, or those with larger portions—and which work well as dinners, thanks to lighter ingredients or smaller serving sizes. I hope this helps you in your Vegan Challenge!

Red and Green Salad

Lunch or Dinner—Better as a dinner option because it's light.

Prep: 10 minutes

½ watermelon radish, sliced thin and cut into bite-sized wedges
4 cherry tomatoes, sliced thin or cut into wedges
1 lunch-sized plate spinach
1 tablespoon dried cranberries
1 tablespoon soaked, dried raw sunflower seeds
Cracked pepper, to taste
1 tablespoon Veganaise (original) or splash Austria's Finest
    Pumpkin Seed Oil

Place spinach on a plate, and place cherry tomatoes, sunflower seeds and dried cranberries on top. Top it all off with a dollop of Veganaise. If you want to go lighter, dress your salad with a splash of Austria's Finest Pumpkin Seed Oil.

Roasted Vegetables

Lunch or Dinner—Better as a lunch option because it's heavier and will take longer to digest.

Your choice of vegetables
Cooking oil
Seasonings (optional)

Cut vegetables into bite-sized pieces and toss in your favorite oil (if you are roasting large vegetables like potatoes or sweet potatoes you can leave them whole; pierce potatoes with a fork before roasting). Toss in enough oil so that all vegetables are coated lightly with the oil and not saturated. Then, toss with your favorite seasonings if desired.

Spread the cut vegetables out in a single layer on a pan. Roast your vegetables at 425°F. Be sure to leave vegetables in the oven until browning takes place to get that perfect roasted taste.

Suggested roasting times (times may vary):
- Beets, carrots, potatoes, onions: 30–45 minutes
- Butternut and acorn squashes: 20–60 minutes
- Brussels sprouts, broccoli, cauliflower: 15–25 minutes
- Tomatoes: 15–20 minutes
- Summer squash, zucchini, asparagus, string beans: 10–20 minutes

Hot Artichoke Dip
Lunch

Prep: 35–40 minutes

1 cup Daiya Mozzarella vegan cheese
1 cup Veganaise original Mayonnaise
1 cup artichoke hearts, finely chopped
Paprika, to taste
Cayenne pepper, to taste (optional)

Preheat oven to 350°F. Combine the first three ingredients in a bowl or in a Pyrex square glass dish. Evenly spread the mixture in a square dish and sprinkle the top of the dish with paprika and cayenne pepper, if desired. Bake until hot and bubbly.

Spaghetti Squash and Greens

Lunch or Dinner—Better as a lunch option because it's heavier and will take longer to digest.

Prep: 50 minutes

Salad greens
1 spaghetti squash
Olive oil (enough to cover spaghetti squash while baking)
Sea salt and cracked pepper, to taste

Preheat oven to 400°F. Cover a jelly roll pan with tin foil. Cut spaghetti squash in half, drizzle with olive oil, and season with sea salt and cracked pepper to taste.

Place upside down on the jelly roll pan. I like to use the jelly roll pan because it has 1-inch sides that keep excess oil from rolling off the pan and into your oven.

Roast spaghetti squash for 45 minutes or until soft and tender. Scoop out the squash, removing any seeds, and place squash on top of greens to serve.

Lisa's Note: *A couple options that I adore with this recipe are placing the greens and roasted spaghetti squash on your plate and then add several spoons of Hot Artichoke Dip (page 87) on top.*

Another option is to place the greens on a plate, followed by roasted spaghetti squash, and mix in Daiya mozzarella cheese, sea salt, cracked pepper and onion or garlic powder, all to taste. You can also add your favorite spaghetti sauce. This is another case where your imagination, your taste buds, and your heritage can make this dish your own.

Sautéed Brussel Sprouts

Lunch or Dinner

Prep: 10 minutes

Brussels sprouts, cut in half
Olive oil
Sea salt, to taste
Daiya mozzarella cheese (optional)

Coat a sauté pan with olive oil and heat. While the pan is heating up, clean the Brussels sprouts and cut in half. Sauté Brussels sprouts until cooked through; I like them slightly dark at the edges. Season with sea salt to taste during the sautéing process.

To add another dimension, sprinkle with Daiya Vegan Mozzarella Cheese until melted. The Brussel sprouts are so good by themselves that they don't need the cheese, but I know many people love to put cheese on everything.

Lisa's Note: *You may wonder why I have sautéed Brussels sprouts as a lunch entry. I know it may sound boring, but I am satisfied with just eating a bowl of sprouts or roasted/unroasted vegetables for lunch. In the early years of my diet/lifestyle change, I thought I needed to have thirty-five options on my plate to keep things interesting and to keep me full. Now my life and my eating has simplified. I eat to live and not live to eat. I'm happy, and I don't feel like I'm missing out on anything. You can also parboil the Brussels sprouts instead of sautéing them.*

Oven-Roasted Butternut Squash

Lunch or Dinner—Better as a lunch option because it's heavier and will take longer to digest.

Prep: 10 minutes
Cook: 25–40 minutes

1 pound butternut squash, cleaned and cut into 1-inch pieces
1 tablespoon olive oil
Sea salt and cracked pepper, to taste

Preheat oven to 350°F, or 450°F for a shorter cooking time.

Toss squash with olive oil in a large bowl and season with sea salt and cracked pepper, to taste. Arrange squash pieces on a large baking sheet. Roast about 25 minutes at 450°F or 35–40 minutes at 350°F or until tender, turning halfway through.

Avocado Toast

Lunch or Dinner—Better as a lunch option because it's heavier and will take longer to digest.

Prep: 10 minutes

Grindstone Bakery Bread (or WrawP Organic Veggie Wrap)
Avocado, sliced
Daiya or your favorite vegan cheese (sliced or shredded)
Sea salt and cracked pepper, to taste (optional)

Toast your favorite Grindstone Bakery Bread and place on a cookie sheet. Layer sliced or shredded vegan cheese on the toast. Place avocado slices on top, and sprinkle with sea salt and cracked pepper, if desired.

Preheat oven to 350°F. Place cookie sheet on middle rack. Bake until cheese melts.

Lisa's Note: *I'm normally allergic to all the usual ingredients in bread, but Grindstone Bakery's bread is organic, whole grain, stone ground, and authentically vegan, using no yeast, no dairy, and no GMOs. It's been a long time since I've been able to find a bread that I could recommend even to bread eaters!*

Grilled Cheese

Lunch or Dinner—Better as a lunch option because it's heavier and will take longer to digest.

Prep: 10 minutes

2 slices Grindstone Bakery Bread
Slices of Daiya or your favorite vegan cheese
Olive oil

Cover sauté or frying pan with olive oil and heat. Build your grilled cheese sandwich by placing bread, layering your favorite vegan cheese, and topping with a final piece of bread. Place sandwich in frying pan. Grill each side until it reaches desired brownness.

Options: You can include other goodies in your grilled cheese sandwich, like sliced tomatoes or slices of Bubbies Raw Pickles.

Lisa's Note: *Grilled cheese is one of the comfort foods that I grew up with. Nothing beats a grilled cheese sandwich and a cup of warm soup on a cold winter's day. Because of my food allergies, I couldn't have a grilled cheese sandwich for about thirty years. Now thanks to Grindstone Bakery, I finally can!*

Family Potato Pancakes

Lunch or Dinner—Better as a lunch option because it's heavier and will take longer to digest.

Prep time: 1 hour
Makes 12 pancakes

2 pounds potatoes, peeled and grated fine
3 tablespoons coconut flour
1 tablespoon egg replacement
Sea salt, to taste

Using either an electric frying pan or a large sauté pan, cover the bottom of pan with olive oil and heat. While the pan is heating, prepare the potatoes. Once the potatoes are peeled and grated, combine all ingredients in a high-speed blender until the batter is well-blended.

Drop 3 tablespoons of the potato mixture into the frying pan at a time. Fry until crispy and golden. Turn and brown the other side. Keep the pancakes warm in a Pyrex glass dish until ready to serve.

Serve with applesauce and jelly. The thickness of the potato pancake is not as thin as a crepe but not as thick as a pancake; it's somewhere in between.

Quinoa Nori Salad

Lunch or Dinner

Prep time: 30 minutes

1/3–½ cup cooked quinoa

¼ slice raw nori sheet cut into ¼ x ½ inch pieces

1 avocado, sliced or cubed

1 tablespoon red onion, chopped

Wheat-free tamari (or soy sauce), to taste

Spritz lemon juice

Mixed spring greens (spinach and sunflower sprouts), enough
to cover plate

Sea salt, to taste

Raw or roasted sunflower seeds or hulled sesame seeds
(optional)

Cooking Quinoa

You can cook your quinoa in an Instant Pot per manufacturer's instructions, or cook in a pot with water and a pinch of salt on your stove top.

When you make quinoa, you first need to determine how much quinoa you want to end up with. Quinoa increases four times in size when cooked, so if you want to end up with 4 cups of cooked quinoa, you need to measure out 1 cup dry quinoa to be cooked. When cooking quinoa, use a 2:1 ratio of water to dry quinoa.

You'll need to wash the quinoa before cooking to remove the bitter coating that protects the seed from being eaten by birds. Although quinoa sold today is usually pre-washed, I still prefer to wash it myself, just to be sure.

Place prewashed quinoa in water per the above ratio. I also add a pinch of sea salt to the water. Some people also flavor the water with coconut sweetener, soy sauce, wheat-free tamari, or vegetable broth.

Simmer in water until the quinoa is softened and chewy and the water is totally absorbed. Cover the pot and stir semi-frequently to make sure the water is absorbed and that the quinoa is not sticking to the pot. Turn the heat off and let the pot sit on top of the stove, covered. The heat captured under the lid helps to make sure the quinoa is totally cooked and has absorbed all of the water.

Assembling the Salad

To build this salad, place the greens and sprouts on your plate, cover with cooked quinoa, and sprinkle on cut up nori sheets and chopped red onions. Next, place cut/sliced avocado and spritz with a touch of lemon juice. Add a pinch of sea salt and drizzle wheat-free tamari, to taste. If you are not allergic to wheat, you can use soy sauce instead of wheat-free tamari.

If you want a little crunch factor, you can sprinkle a handful of raw or roasted sunflower seeds.

THE RECIPES

Three Nut Basil Pesto Pasta

Lunch or Dinner

Prep: 10–15 minutes
Prep (Pesto): 10 minutes

4 medium zucchini, spiralized

Toppings:
Cherry tomatoes, quartered or whole (quantity as desired)—
    approximately ½-1 cup
6 asparagus stalks, thinly sliced on an angle
½ cup fresh chopped cilantro

Pesto:
2 cups raw pine nuts
½ cup raw cashews
½ cup raw macadamia nuts
4 garlic cloves, minced
6 tablespoons fresh lemon juice
2 teaspoons Himalayan sea salt
1 cup fresh basil, chopped

Pasta:
Spiralize zucchini and set aside.

Pesto:
Combine ingredients in a food processor until well blended and set aside.

Now it's time to build your dish. Place the zucchini in a large bowl and combine with the pesto and top with the cherry tomatoes, asparagus, and cilantro. Alternately, you can serve all parts of the recipe separately, so when you have guests over you allow them to build the dish themselves! Place the zucchini on a plate (of greens, if desired), add a spoonful of pesto (amount depends on how much they like pesto), and top with the tomatoes, asparagus, and cilantro.

Lisa's Note: *Spiralizing helps you to diversify your meal. For example, spiralized zucchini can act as your vegetable spaghetti. You can then sauté it in a frying pan, adding tomatoes, garlic, and whatever other vegetables you are in the mood for. Or, as in this recipe, you can spiralize the zucchini and add it cold.*

Spiralizing also lets you add a rainbow of color to almost any dish. Spiralize different colored vegetables like yams and red beets and turn them into a salad, or just have fun and spiralize whatever you have in the house (like zucchini, yellow squash, red beets, and yams). With all those colors included, not only is it good for you, but it's so pleasing to the eye.

THE RECIPES

Ratatouille

Lunch or Dinner—Better as a lunch option because it's heavier and will take longer to digest; if eaten for dinner, use smaller portions.

Prep: 40 minutes

16 ounces Roma tomatoes
1 yellow squash, chopped
1 zucchini, chopped
1 red bell pepper, chopped
1 yellow pepper, chopped
1 orange pepper, chopped
1 eggplant, cubed
1–2 large Portobello mushrooms, chopped
1 red onion, chopped or ringed
2 cloves garlic, minced
2 teaspoons dried parsley
2 teaspoons dried oregano
2 tablespoons olive oil
½ cup orange juice
Sea salt, to taste
Ground pepper, to taste

Pulse-chop tomatoes in food processor so they look like stewed tomatoes and set aside. Chop remaining vegetables and combine with tomatoes in a large mixing bowl. Add seasonings to mixture and coat thoroughly. Add more olive oil if necessary to make sure all vegetables are coated.

You can either place the ingredients in a glass baking dish and bake at 350°F until vegetables are cooked to desired consistency, or you can sauté in a sauté pan until desired consistency.

Toasted Sesame Mayo

Prep: 7 minutes

1 cup raw cashews
½ cup water
½ teaspoon sea salt
1 teaspoon lemon juice
½ teaspoon agave
½ teaspoon toasted sesame oil
1 teaspoon black sesame seeds

Combine all ingredients (except black sesame seeds) in a high-speed blender until creamy-smooth. Pour mayo mixture into a bowl and stir in the black sesame seeds with a spoon.

Lisa's Note: *I use this as a dressing, a spread on raw crackers, and as a dip with crudités. I also use this as a filler in wraps, whether it be nori, wraps, or lettuce/collard leaf wraps.*

THE RECIPES

Basic Mayo

Prep: 7 minutes

1 cup raw cashews
½ cup water
½ teaspoon sea salt
1 teaspoon freshly squeezed lemon juice
½ teaspoon agave

Blend all ingredients in a Vitamix® High Speed Blender or food processor until creamy-smooth. This works great as a dressing, a spread on crackers, as a dip, or as fillers for assorted wraps.

Olive Tapenade

Prep: 7 minutes

1 cup pitted olives
1 tablespoon cold-pressed olive oil
½ teaspoon lemon juice
1 Medjool date

Combine the above ingredients in your Vitamix® High Speed Blender or food processor. Store in Ball® jar with lid in your refrigerator. Tapenade is great as a cracker topping, topping on your salad, or filler in a wrap or nori roll.

This works great as a snack on crackers, sprinkled on top of salads, on vegetables, in soups, or as an add-on in wraps.

Nori Rolls
Lunch or Dinner

Prep: 30 minutes

Filling
3 tablespoons white miso
¼–½ teaspoon toasted sesame oil

Assembly
Raw nori sheets
Assorted vegetables, thinly sliced

Filling
Combine the miso and toasted sesame oil and set aside. This keeps in a sealed container for a week.

Assembly
Spread the filling on a raw nori sheet which you lay out (shiny side down) on a bamboo sushi mat. Spread the miso filling over the first inch of the nori sheet. Then fill with your favorite vegetables (such as carrots, celery, cucumber, mushrooms, onion, sprouts, red pepper, and avocados). Lay the thinly sliced vegetables across the nori sheet then roll up, starting with the end closest to you.

Seal the end of the nori roll with water. Cut the long nori roll into 1-inch pieces. I use wheat-free tamari as a dipping sauce.

Lisa's Note: *My Toasted Sesame Mayo (page 99), Basic Mayo (page 100), or Olive Tapenade" (page 101) can enhance a salad, top a spiralized vegetable, or be used as part of a filler when making nori rolls.*

Unstir Fry

Lunch or Dinner—Better as a lunch option because it's heavier and will take longer to digest. If eaten for dinner, use smaller portions.

1 cup shitake mushrooms, sliced

1½ pounds assorted vegetables (miniature corn cobs, chopped red onions, carrot sticks, mung bean sprouts, red/yellow pepper slices, snow peas, etc.)

Stir Fry Marinade

¼ cup sesame oil

⅓ cup wheat free tamari

¼ cup toasted sesame oil

¼ cup Austria's Finest, Naturally® pumpkin seed oil

Sea salt, to taste

In a sauté pan, sauté the marinated vegetables until heated to your liking. Or, you can bake in an oven at 350°F in a glass baking dish until heated to your satisfaction.

Baked Sweet Potatoes
Lunch or Dinner

Prep: 15 minutes

2 sweet potatoes, peeled and grated
1 carrot, peeled and shredded
1 apple, cored and shredded
1 tablespoon alcohol-free vanilla
Raisins (optional)
Shredded coconut (optional)
Cinnamon, to taste
Agave, to taste

Place shredded sweet potatoes, apple, and carrots in a glass casserole dish. Sprinkle with cinnamon to taste, add vanilla, and cover with agave. Make sure the sweet potatoes are totally covered with the cinnamon, vanilla, and agave mixture.

Place in glass dish or lay on a foil-covered baking pan and bake at 350°F until cooked through.

Roasted Red Pepper and Asparagus

Lunch or Dinner

Prep: 15 minutes

1 bunch asparagus
1 red pepper, cleaned and diced
¼–½ cup Austria's Finest, Naturally® pumpkin seed oil
Sea salt and cracked black pepper, to taste

Cut asparagus on an angle into bite-size pieces. Be sure to remove hard tips and discard. Place cleaned and sliced asparagus and red pepper in a glass dish. Toss and cover with pumpkin seed oil. Season with sea salt and black pepper to taste.

Place glass dish in an oven and bake at 350°F until cooked to your satisfaction.

Sauerkraut
Lunch or Dinner

Prep: 30 minutes
Ferment: 3–5 days in summer, up to 2 weeks in winter

Red and green cabbages
Radishes
Daikon
Onion
Herbs such as parsley, dill, and scallions, to taste (I personally throw in a few handfuls)
Spiralized vegetables such as beets, yellow squash, yams, and zucchini
Sea salt

Shred all vegetables. Combine all ingredients in a bowl. For every quart of ingredients, add a tablespoon of sea salt. Mix it together, place in a canning jar, and pack it tightly, leaving approximately 1 inch of space at the top of the jar (it is important to leave this space because when you keep packing down the vegetables, the liquid will rise).

Cover it with two pieces of cheesecloth and use a rubber band or the ring for the canning jar to hold the cheesecloth in place. Set the jar on your countertop. Twice a day, take off the ring and cheesecloth and with clean hands, keep pushing down on the vegetables (the liquid continues to rise to the top and will eventually evaporate).

In the summer, the sauerkraut will ferment in 3–7 days, depending on your local temperature. In the winter, it will take a few weeks. Once it has fermented, place the lid on the canning jar and store it in your refrigerator.

I use sauerkraut as an add-on to a salad or as a filler in my nori rolls. It's so good for you. (Or you could just eat sauerkraut straight because it tastes sooo good!)

Happy Harvest Salad

Lunch or Dinner—Works well as a dinner option, since it's lighter.

Prep: 20 minutes

4 large tomatoes, chopped
¼ cup red onion, diced
3 cloves garlic, chopped
3 ears fresh corn, removed from cob
¼ cup basil, chiffonade
1 tablespoon Austria's Finest Naturally® Pumpkin Seed Oil
1 teaspoon Himalayan sea salt
Pinch cracked black pepper

Combine the above ingredients in a bowl, toss, and enjoy. I think this salad actually tastes better the next day. On the first day, the basil can sometimes taste overpowering, but when the flavors have an opportunity to meld overnight, the flavors are balanced and really delicious.

Seaweed and Shitake Salad

Lunch or Dinner—Works well as a dinner option, since it's lighter.

Prep: 20 minutes

2 cups dried seaweed (hiziki or sea palm are my favorites)
1 cup shitake mushrooms, finely sliced
2 garlic cloves, minced
Pinch of sea salt
Pinch freshly ground black pepper
2 tablespoons cold-pressed olive oil
1 teaspoon wheat-free tamari
¼ teaspoon toasted sesame oil

Soak the seaweed in cold water until water is absorbed and sea vegetables have been rehydrated. Pour off water. In a separate bowl, whisk together remaining ingredients. Pour dressing over the sea vegetables. You can eat as is or place in glass bowl and dehydrate at 105°F to heat the salad and/or meld the flavors. I add seaweed salad on top of a green salad. I also use it as part of filler in a wrap. You can eat it as is, or with a spoonful of the toasted sesame mayo on top.

Very Basic Hummus
Lunch or Dinner

Prep: 15 minutes

1¼ soaked and sprouted chickpeas
1 cup tahini paste
4 cloves garlic, crushed
½ cup parsley
2 tablespoons agave
3 teaspoons sea salt
4 tablespoons lemon juice
¼ cup water
¼ cup cold-pressed olive oil

Combine the above ingredients in a food processor or high speed blender until desired smoothness. If you wish for your hummus to be even smoother, you can add a little more water and or oil (or both).

You can use the hummus as a dip, in a wrap along with vegetables cut in sticks and greens, or as the filler with vegetables in nori rolls.

Collard Wrap
Lunch or Dinner

Prep: 10 minutes

Very Basic Hummus, see page 109
Assorted vegetables cut in long sticks, (carrots, celery, pepper,
    tomatoes, avocado wedges, mushrooms)
Sprouts

Place your collard wrap on the counter; fill with hummus, sprouts,
and assorted vegetables; and roll it up. You can pick this up and eat
it like a sandwich, or you can cut it. I tend to cut mine; otherwise
I end up wearing it.

Cooked Wild Rice and Chickpea Salad

Lunch or Dinner—Better as a lunch, as rice is harder to digest.

Prep: 20 minutes

2 cups natural wilderness rice

1½ cups chickpeas, sprouted and pulse-chopped in food
    processor to desired consistency

2 teaspoons ground cumin seeds

1 medium red onion, chopped

2½ tablespoons cold-pressed olive oil

2 teaspoons cumin powder

1½ teaspoons curry powder

⅔ cup dried blueberries or raisins

2 tablespoons parsley, chopped

1 tablespoon cilantro (If you don't like cilantro, replace with
    extra parsley)

1 tablespoon dill, chopped

Salt and ground black pepper, to taste

You will need an Instant Pot for this recipe.

Your chickpeas can be sprouted, or you can use a can of chickpeas, draining the liquid or using it as part of the 2.5 cups water called for to cook the ingredients in the Instant Pot.

Place the rice, ingredients and water in an Instant Pot and set it to cook for 22 minutes pressure cooking time. When the time is up, open the cooker using the 10-minute Natural Pressure Release (see Instant Pot directions).

THE RECIPES

Mediterranean Dressing

From Angeline Ritter of Just Vegan

This dressing is delicious, nutritional, vegan, and stays fresh in your refrigerator until it's time for your next salad or sandwich topping.

2 cups extra virgin olive oil

½ cup balsamic vinegar

½ cup red wine vinegar

2 tablespoons Dijon mustard

1 tablespoon dry oregano

1 tablespoon dry basil

2 teaspoons garlic powder

2 teaspoons onion powder

1½ teaspoon Himalayan sea salt

½ teaspoon black pepper

Place all ingredients in a blender and blend until mixed. Store dressing in an airtight container and place in the refrigerator. When ready to use, shake and serve.

Note: this dressing might solidify in refrigerator. If you take it out of refrigerator 15 minutes before serving, it will liquefy nicely.

Chipotle Mayo

From Angeline Ritter of Just Vegan

This dressing/spread has a spicy zip but is not too hot to enjoy! You can raise the heat by increasing the hot sauces.

2 cups avocado mayonnaise

3 tablespoons fire-roasted pepper salsa

2 tablespoons sriracha hot sauce

2 tablespoons crystal hot sauce

2 tablespoons tapatio hot sauce

Place all ingredients in a blender and blend until mixed. Store spread in an airtight container and place in refrigerator. When ready to use, shake and serve.

GBG'S (Grains, Beans and Greens)

From Brenda Hinton
Lunch or Dinner—As beans tend to be heavier and harder to digest,
better to eat this earlier in the day.

Yield: Varies

Grains
White or brown rice
Lentils
Quinoa
Potatoes

Beans
Black beans
White (Great Northern)
    beans
Garbanzo beans
Red kidney beans

Greens
Lettuce
Kale
Spinach
Chard

Sauce
Any nut-based sauce
    or dressing

Prepare ingredients as desired and set aside.

This recipe is intended to be customized and customizable. The ingredients listed above are only suggestions; you can include all or none of them, in whatever amounts suit your needs.

A few suggestions that are a big hit in my household:

Greek GBG: Quinoa, garbanzo beans, romaine lettuce. Add: sliced Kalamata olives, tomatoes, and red onion slices, and use a mustard vinaigrette or Greek salad dressing as your sauce.

Mexican GBG: Small white potatoes, quinoa or rice, black or kidney beans, romaine lettuce. Add: sliced olives, tomatoes, mild chiles, and top with avocado slices and salsa.

Classic GBG: Grain/quinoa, any beans (small white ones are nice), any greens (spinach is a favorite) and top with sauce.

Golden Paste

From Brenda Hinton

As an animal lover, a rescue dog is always part of my life. I've learned so much from them as they age, leading me to fine-tune meal prep, adopting natural remedies and complementary healing modalities. Truly, "food is medicine!"

½ cup turmeric powder

1 cup water + 1 cup water in reserve, if needed

⅓ cups unrefined coconut/flaxseed-linseed oil, virgin/extra virgin olive oil

2–3 teaspoons freshly ground black pepper

Place turmeric and water in pan, stirring over gentle heat until you have a thick paste. This should take about 7–10 minutes, and you may need to add additional water along the way.

Add freshly ground pepper and oil at the end of cooking. Stir well (a whisk is ideal) to incorporate the oil and allow to cool.

This recipe keeps for 2 weeks if refrigerated. Freeze a portion if you think you have too much to use within two weeks. Thaw in the refrigerator when needed.

Note: This is a wonderful paste to add to a cup or so of hot water for turmeric tea or add to warm milk (coconut, almond, or similar) with some cinnamon, stevia, or your favorite sweetener for Golden Milk as an evening tonic.

THE RECIPES

Quinoa Enchilada Casserole

From Brenda Hinton

Lunch or Dinner—Better as a lunch option because it's heavier and will take longer to digest.

Quinoa has become a versatile part of many vegan kitchens. Actually a seed, not a grain, quinoa is ideal added warm to bowls and cold to greens and other components, making a hearty full meal salad or cooked into casseroles for nourishing dinner alternatives.

Yield: One 9 x 11 casserole dish

1 cup quinoa, cooked
1 can enchilada sauce (10–15 oz)
1 can, chopped green chiles (4.5 oz)
1 can black beans (15 oz)
1 cup corn kernels
2 tablespoons cilantro, chopped
1 teaspoon cumin
1 teaspoon chili powder
Salt and pepper, to taste
1 cup vegan cheddar cheese, shredded
1 cup vegan Mozzarella cheese, shredded
1 can sliced olives
1 avocado, sliced
1–2 Roma tomatoes, chopped (or cherry tomatoes cut in ½)

Preheat the oven to 375°F. Cook quinoa as directed and set aside.

Lightly oil a 9 x 11 casserole dish. In a large bowl, combine the first nine ingredients and stir in ½ cup each of the vegan cheddar and vegan Mozzarella cheese. Spread the resulting mixture in the dish and top with the remaining vegan cheese.

Bake for 30 minutes at 375°F. Top with olives, avocado and tomatoes, and serve.

Quinoa Tabbouleh

From Brenda Hinton

Lunch or Dinner

Tabbouleh is another Middle Eastern dish I have always enjoyed. Adding quinoa, my favorite grain replacement, in place of bulgur is a tasty alternative. You might consider doubling the recipe to have some around for snacking later!

Yield: Approximately 3 cups

1 cup quinoa

1½ cups water

1 cup halved cherry tomatoes (or 2–3 medium fresh
   tomatoes, diced)

3 scallions, green parts only, thinly sliced

½ cup minced parsley

½ cup, chopped black olives

Juice of 1 lemon

1 tablespoon olive oil

Salt and pepper, to taste

¼ cup toasted pumpkin or sunflower seeds (for garnish)

¼–½ cup mint, minced (optional)

Cook quinoa in water as directed. Fluff and transfer to a medium size bowl. Allow to cool before adding the remaining ingredients and toss gently until well combined.

Sprinkle pumpkin or sunflower seeds on top and serve at room temperature. Store in a sealed glass container in the refrigerator for up to one week.

Baked Avocado with Cherry Tomatoes

From Heidi Albertsen
Lunch or Dinner—Works well as a dinner option, as it's lighter.

100 grams cherry tomatoes
4 ripe avocados
4–5 garlic cloves
3 teaspoons white truffle oil (organic)
2 limes, juiced
Handful of coriander
Extra virgin olive oil
Sesame oil
Avocado oil
Vegan parmesan cheese (optional)
Salt and pepper, to taste

Preheat the oven to 350°F. Clean the tomatoes before cutting them into halves. Cut the avocados in halves, removing the seeds. Place the avocado halves on a baking tray and drizzle a little olive oil so that they don't stick while baking.

Place the tomatoes into a bowl, adding salt and pepper to taste. Add the truffle oil and stir gently.

Place the tomatoes into the avocado halves where the seeds used to be and drizzle with tiny bit of sesame oil and avocado oil. You can also sprinkle on some parmesan cheese, if you'd like.

Bake for 15–20 minutes. Once the dish is ready to serve, add the coriander for garnish and enjoy!

Broccoli Salad with Tahini Sauce

From Heidi Albertsen
Lunch or Dinner—Works well as a dinner option, as it's lighter.

Prep: 15 minutes

300 grams broccoli, cut in small bouquets
200 grams snow peas
1 big red onion, thinly sliced
3 tablespoons coriander, chopped
2 tablespoons peanuts, chopped

Sauce
2 rounded tablespoons tahini paste
1 crushed garlic clove
1 tablespoon soy sauce
Juice of 1 lime
1 rounded tablespoon agave
Salt and pepper, to taste

Place the broccoli, snow peas, and red onions on a big plate. Mix tahini paste, garlic, soy sauce, lime juice, agave, salt, and pepper. Dress the salad with the creamy tahini sauce and top with coriander and peanuts.

Cashew Spread

From Heidi Albertsen

Yield: One small glass

200 grams raw cashews
1–2 garlic cloves
2 tablespoons white wine vinegar
1 tablespoon lemon juice
1–2 tablespoonful chives, chopped
Sea salt, to taste

Soak the cashews overnight. Blend the soaked and drained cashews and the garlic in a food processor until they're very finely chopped. Add vinegar, lemon juice, and salt and blend until it tastes and looks good. Add the chopped chives and set aside to cool. This can last 2–3 days in the refrigerator

Make sure the cashews you're soaking haven't already been roasted. The cashews need to be raw.

Zucchini, Carrot, and Cucumber Salad

From Heidi Albertsen
Lunch or Dinner—Works well as a dinner option, as it's light and refreshing.

Prep time: 15 minutes

2 zucchini
3 large carrots
1 large German cucumber
Handful pumpkin seeds (organic)
Handful sunflower seeds (organic)
4 tablespoons cold first pressed olive oil
2 tablespoons apple cider vinegar
1 teaspoon paprika
Sea salt and pepper, to taste

Use a vegetable peeler to peel the zucchini, carrots and cucumber into strips. Peel and discard the outer layer of the zucchini, carrots, and cucumbers first; I find it hard to peel the very center of each veggie, so feel free to discard (or nibble) this so that you don't end up peeling your fingers!

Place the strips of zucchini, carrots, and cucumber in a bowl with the seeds. Pour the oil and vinegar over them, then sprinkle the paprika, salt, and pepper on top. Stir everything well. It will keep, covered, in a fridge for up to 3 days.

Dirty Chocolate Cake

From Heidi Albertsen
Lunch or Dinner
This amazingly soft chocolate cake is easy to make and very good
for serving to guests.

Serves: 8–10 people

200 grams soft Medjool
    pitted dates
55 grams raw cacao
100 grams cashews
100 grams walnuts (soaked
    walnuts)
25 grams coconut butter
    (Lupak Danish Butter)
Pinch sea salt
25 grams Gogi Berries

Toppings
175 grams dark chocolate
2 deciliters soya milk
400 grams silk tofu
Fresh berries

Soak the raw cashews and walnuts overnight, making sure to drain off the water afterwards. Blend dates, raw cacao, cashews, walnuts, and coconut oil together in a food processor. Add sea salt and Gojii berries and blend again.

Place the dough, nice and neatly, into an oven form and put in the refrigerator for a least one hour.

Toppings
Chop the dark chocolate and add it to a bowl. Warm the soya milk and pour it over the chocolate, steeping it as it melts. Add the silk tofu in a second bowl, then add the chocolate. Remove the dough from the fridge and add the chocolate mousse topping.

Return the cake to the refrigerator for least two hours, or overnight. Serve the cake topped with berries.

This cake can keep for three days in the refrigerator.

Grilled Tasty Vegetables

Heidi Albertsten
Lunch or Dinner

4 beet roots, chopped into bite-size pieces
4 carrots, peeled and cut into bite-size pieces
2 parsnips, cut into bite-size pieces
4 bell peppers, cut into bite-size pieces
Salt and pepper, to taste
Basil and fresh coriander, to taste
Olive oil

Preheat the oven to 350–400°F. Place beetroot, bell peppers, carrots, parsnips, and peppers onto an oven tray. Add fresh coriander, basil, parsley, salt, pepper, and a drizzle of olive oil. Make sure the vegetables are coated thoroughly with herbs and olive oil.

Bake for 30–45 minutes until desired doneness.

Healthy Minestrone Soup

Lunch or Dinner—Works well as a dinner option, as it's lighter.
This colorful soup—full of healthy veggies like carrots, leeks, and
asparagus—can be prepped in a mere 20 minutes!

Yield: 4 servings

2 tablespoons olive oil

2 medium carrots, chopped and peeled

1 medium leek, thinly sliced

8 sprigs fresh thyme, tied together

3 large red potatoes, chopped

2 quart low-sodium vegetable broth

1 bunch asparagus, sliced

1 can (15 oz.) navy beans, rinsed and drained (optional)

2 tablespoons fresh dill, chopped

In an 8-quart saucepot, heat 2 tablespoons olive oil on medium heat. Add carrots, leek, fresh thyme, and ¼ teaspoon salt. Cook 8 minutes, stirring occasionally.

Add red potatoes and vegetable broth. Partially cover and heat to boiling on high, before reducing heat to a simmer. Cook 25 minutes or until potatoes are tender.

Add asparagus and simmer 3 minutes, or until tender. Discard thyme and stir in navy beans (optional), fresh dill, ¼ teaspoon salt, and 1/2 teaspoon pepper.

Heaven Soup

Heidi Albertsen
Lunch or Dinner—Works well as a dinner option, as it's lighter.

Prep: 20 minutes

1 cucumber, unpeeled and cut into small pieces
1 red bell pepper, seeded and cored, cut in to small pieces
2 celery stalks, julienned
1 medium tomato
¼ cup red onion, chopped
1 apple, cored and chopped
1-inch knob fresh ginger root, minced
3 garlic cloves, peeled and minced
1–2 bushy sprigs fresh cilantro, chopped finely
¼ cup freshly squeezed lemon juice
2½ cups distilled water
2 heaping tablespoons unpasteurized miso
¼ Bragg liquid amino

Combine ingredients in a large pot on a stove and bring to a boil.
Simmer until ingredients are cooked through.

Sautéed Hiziki with Spring Vegetables

From Heidi Albertsen
Lunch or Dinner

¼ cup dried hiziki

2 spring onions (both white and green parts), cut in thin
   diagonals

3 carrots, cut into matchsticks

3–4 cups sugar snap peas

¼ cup water

1½ tablespoon nama shoyu (or wheat-free tamari)

1 tablespoon toasted sesame oil

Soak hiziki in water for 15 minutes, or until soft. In a frying pan, add water and sauté onion for 1–2 minutes. Add hiziki, carrots, and ½ cup of water and sauté for 7–10 minutes.

Add sugar snap peas, toasted sesame oil, and nama shoyu or wheat-free tamari and continue cooking 2–3 minutes.

Steamed Cruciferous Vegetables with Tangy Tahini Dressing

From Heidi Albertsen
Lunch or Dinner

Yields: 4 servings

½ head cauliflower florets
1 broccoli stalk, florets and stem
4 tablespoons sesame tahini
1½ tablespoon maple syrup
Juice of 1 lemon
2–3 tablespoons shoyu
½ cup water

Place water in a pot with steamer basket. Add cauliflower florets; cover and bring to a high heat. Cook 5–7 minutes or until cauliflower is tender. Repeat with the broccoli.

In a food process or blender, combine tahini, maple syrup, lemon juice, shoyu, and water. Top steamed cauliflower and broccoli with tahini dressing and serve.

Creamy Carrot Soup with Potato

From Heidi Albertsen
Lunch or Dinner—Works well as a dinner option, as it's lighter.

Yields: Approximately 6 cups

2 tablespoons extra virgin olive oil
1 large onion (about ¾ pound), cut into medium-sized cubes
½ teaspoon sea salt
2 pounds carrots, peeled and cut into ½-inch rounds
5 cups water
½ medium potato (about ¼ pound), peeled and cut into
    medium chunks
1 teaspoon lemon juice
1½ teaspoon ginger juice

In a medium pot, heat oil over medium heat. Add onions and salt and sweat until onions are softened (about 5–8 minutes). Stir often to prevent browning.

Add the carrots, cover the pot, and cook over low heat for 5–6 minutes, stirring to prevent browning. Add water and potatoes to pot. Raise the heat and bring to a boil. Reduce heat to low and simmer 25 minutes, covered, until carrots are very tender.

Blend the soup until creamy, adding additional stock to reach desired consistency. Add lemon and ginger juice. Readjust seasonings to taste and serve.

Baked Quinoa

From Heidi Albertsen

Lunch or Dinner—Better as a lunch option because it's heavier and will take longer to digest.

Yield: 3 cups

1 cup quinoa, washed and drained
1 tablespoon + 1 teaspoon extra virgin olive oil
1¼ cups boiling water
½ teaspoon salt

Preheat oven to 350°F. Place quinoa in a small baking pan and roast about 20 minutes, or until quinoa is dry. Add 1 tablespoon oil and stir into the quinoa. Cook 5 minutes more, stirring once or twice.

Add water and ½ teaspoon salt to quinoa. Tightly cover with foil and bake 20 minutes, or until all water is absorbed. Remove from oven and let sit covered for 5 minutes. Remove foil and fluff with fork. Place quinoa into a bowl and let cool.

Quick Quinoa with Cilantro Pesto

From Heidi Albertsen
Lunch or Dinner

Yield: 4–6 servings

1 cup quinoa
2 cups water
Pinch sea salt
½ bunch cilantro, cleaned
1-inch ginger, peeled and minced
¼ cup extra virgin olive oil
2–3 tablespoons rice vinegar

Rinse quinoa in a large bowl with cold water. Discard any grains that float to the top of the rinsing bowl. Bring quinoa and 2 cups water to a boil. Add a pinch of sea salt and lower heat to simmer. Cover and cook 12–15 minutes or until all the water evaporates.

Combine cilantro, ginger, olive oil, rice vinegar, and ½ teaspoon sea salt in a food processor or blender. Pulse until smooth and creamy. Toss cooked quinoa with cilantro pesto.

Creamy Carob Mousse

From Heidi Albertsen
Lunch or Dinner
The first time I ate an avocado mousse, I was shocked! How could the same avocado which makes my favorite guacamole also make my most favorite dessert? I can't explain—you'll just need to try it for yourself.

Serves: 2

2 avocados
1 tablespoon alcohol extract
1 teaspoon sea salt
5 deglet dates

Soak the avocados in water for 3 hours. Discard the soaking water afterwards.

In the bowl of a food processor, use the S blade to blend all the ingredients until creamy. Add water as needed if a lighter consistency is desired. Divide among individual serving dishes and chill until needed.

Quinoa Porridge with Grilled Zucchini

From Heidi Albertsen
Lunch or Dinner

6 tablespoons oil, divided
3 cloves garlic, finely chopped
300 grams quinoa
1.2 liters vegetable stock
4 tablespoons parsley, chopped
2 tablespoons pine nuts
300 grams zucchini
Salt and pepper, to taste

Heat 2 tablespoons oil in a deep frying pan and add garlic. After a minute or two, add quinoa and vegetable stock. Stir and let cook over medium heat for 25 minutes.

Put 2 tablespoons oil, parsley, pine nuts, salt, and pepper into a blender and chop until creamy.

Cut the zucchini into two halves before slicing in 5 mm pieces. Heat 2 tablespoons oil in a frying pan and add the zucchini. Cook until golden. Add salt and peppers.

Serve the porridge in bowls, topping with zucchini and pesto.

Superfood Kale Avocado Salad with Raw Olives

From Heidi Albertsen
Lunch or Dinner
This recipe is simple, versatile, and packed with detoxifying greens and nutrient-dense superfoods. You can vary the type of greens, sprouts, herbs, and veggies according to what is in season. As far as superfoods go, the more the better!

Prep: 15–20 minutes
Serves: 1–2

1 head kale
¼ teaspoons salt
1 lemon, squeezed
1 tomato, chopped
½ carrot, chopped
½ avocado
¼ cup black botija olives, pitted and chopped
¼ cup fresh dulse
Handful sprouts
Handful goji berries
Handful fresh herbs
Handful raw cashews

Remove the stems from the kale and place in a large bowl. Put salt on the leaves and start massaging them until the salt starts to "cook" the leaves, i.e., break down the leaves so that they are wilted.

Next, massage the leaves with lemon juice. Finally, massage the leaves with avocado until well incorporated. Taste to determine whether you need more lemon juice or salt.

Place it in a serving bowl and add the rest of ingredients, tossing to combine.

Twelve Superfoods Salad

From Heidi Albertsen (and her friend Chef Louisa Lorange)
Lunch or Dinner—Better as a lunch option because many ingredients make it heavier.

Serves: 2
Prep: 25 minutes
Cook Time: 15 minutes

½ cup dry quinoa

½ cup frozen edamame

½ bunch curly kale (about 4–5 cups), chopped or torn into bite-sized pieces with thick ribs removed

½ cup fresh blueberries

½ cup red grapes, halved

½ cup dried cherries, chopped if necessary (dried cranberries may be substituted)

⅓ cups vegan feta, goat, or parmesan cheese, crumbled or shredded

¼ cup sunflower seeds

¼ cup walnuts, chopped

¼ cup orange juice

2 tablespoons olive oil

1 garlic clove, finely minced or pressed

1 teaspoon agave

½ teaspoon salt, or to taste

¼ teaspoon pepper, or to taste

1 heaping tablespoon Veganiase or vegan Greek yogurt

Cook quinoa according to package directions. Transfer about half the cooked quinoa to a very large bowl.

Cook edamame according to package directions. Drain and add to the bowl.

To the bowl, add the kale, blueberries, grapes, dried cherries, vegan cheese, sunflower seeds, and walnuts and stir to combine; set aside.

To a glass mason jar with a lid, add the orange juice, olive oil, garlic, salt, and pepper. Seal with lid and shake vigorously to combine, about 1–2 minutes.

Add the vegan Greek yogurt and shake until creamy and incorporated, about 1 minute. Taste and check for seasoning balance, adding more salt, pepper, etc. as necessary.

Add desired amount of dressing to salad, toss well to combine, and serve immediately. Extra dressing will keep airtight in the fridge for up to 1 week; shake vigorously before using.

Vegan Quesadillas

Lunch or Dinner—Better as a lunch option because it's heavier and will take longer to digest.

Serves: 3–4

Cheese
400 grams potato
1 large carrot
1 onion
3 pieces garlic
½–1 cup boiled water (for the vegetables)
1 deciliter cashews
½ cup vegan sour cream (or Veganaise)
2 teaspoon baking powder
1 pinch paprika
1 teaspoon lemon juice
Salt, to taste

Quesadillas
6–8 tortillas
Handful baby spinach

Toppings
1 romaine or two mini romaine leaves, finely chopped
2 tomatoes, cut in small bits
1 jalapeno, cut into small pieces
2 cans boiled black beans
2 avocados, chopped
4–5 radishes
Coriander
Lime, cut into slices
Chili sauce

Cheese
Peel the potatoes, carrots, onion, and garlic, and cut them into small pieces. Boil the water in a bowl and add the potato, carrots, onions, and garlic until they're well done. Reserve the water and leave the vegetables to cool. Blend cashews, soya cream, and the boiling water from the vegetables in the food processor until it's nice and smooth.

Blend vegetables together with the cashews, adding a little water if necessary. Add the baking powder, paprika, salt, and lemon juice.

Quesadillas

Add the tortillas to a warm pan. Add cheese and spinach and lightly warm the tortilla. Flip the tortilla after a few minutes and move to a plate. Top with salad, tomato, jalapeno beans, avocado, and coriander. Drizzle with some lime juice and spice it up with some salt. Serve right away with sliced lime and chili sauce.

Mediterranean Layer Pie

Lunch or Dinner—Better as a lunch option because it's heavier and will take longer to digest. If you eat for dinner, reduce your portion size.

Quinoa
1½ cup white quinoa
1½ cup pure water
1 sweet onion, chopped well
1 teaspoon coconut oil
Pinch salt and pepper

Almond Nut Spread
4 cup slivered almonds
½ cup nutritional yeast
2 lemons (juice only)
1½ teaspoons sea salt
1 cup pure water

Tomato Supreme Medley
6 pints cherry tomato,
    sliced in halves (or
    chopped very lightly in
    food processor)
2 cup basil (ribbon cut;
    stack the basil and roll,
    then slice)
1 bunch Italian parsley,
    chopped fine
6 cloves garlic, chopped
1 teaspoon crushed red chili
    pepper
2 jalapeño peppers,
    chopped very small

Vegan Parmesan (for Topping)
2 cups hemp seeds
2 cups nutritional yeast
2 teaspoons sea salt
1 teaspoon crushed red
    chili pepper, or more to
    taste
6 tablespoons olive oil

Quinoa
Soak the quinoa overnight. Rinse well the next day, once you're ready to steam cook.

Add all the ingredients to a 2-quart pot. Bring to a boil and cover with a lid and steam cook, then set aside.

Almond Nut Spread
Purée all ingredients in a Vitamix blender or food processor until it has a creamy consistency, then set aside.

Tomato Supreme Medley
Mix all ingredients together in bowl and set aside until needed.

Assembling the pie
Preheat oven to 350°F. In a medium to large baking pan (at least 5 inches deep), layer the quinoa, almond nut spread (pat it in using a rubber spatula), and tomato medley.

Warm for 20 minutes before serving. Serve with Vegan Parmesan and drizzle with cold pressed olive oil.

Vegan Thai Curry

From Heidi Albertsen
Lunch or Dinner—if you eat this at dinner, reduce your portion size.

Serves: 4
Time: 45 minutes

1 onion
2 garlic cloves
1 tablespoon Thai green curry paste
400 ml can of coconut milk
1 teaspoon maple syrup
1 lemongrass stalk, bashed
1 tablespoon tamari
Handful fresh basil leaves, chopped
1 red chili, chopped
3 zucchini, cut into bite-sized pieces
175 g baby corn, cut into bite-sized pieces
Salt and pepper, to taste
Squeeze lemon juice
Olive oil

Start by chopping the onion and garlic and placing them in a pan over medium heat with a drizzle of olive oil. Cook for 8–10 minutes, or until soft.

Once your onions are soft, spoon in your curry paste and stir well. Cook for another few minutes before adding coconut milk. Bring the whole thing to the boil, then add lemon grass, maple syrup, lemon juice, tamari, zucchini, and baby corn. Reduce the temperature and let simmer for 25–30 minutes.

Once everything is cooked through, remove the lemon grass stalk and serve with a sprinkle of chopped basil leaves, chili, salt, and pepper.

Warm Zucchini Noodle Red Pepper Spice Roast

Lunch or Dinner—Better as a lunch option because it's heavier and will take longer to digest.

Prep: 1 hour

4 large zucchini (spiralized into pasta noodles)
2 red peppers, sliced thin
1 red pepper, chopped
6 garlic cloves
2 jalapeño chili
2 shallots, sliced thin
1 sweet onion
½ red onion
6 small purple potatoes, sliced in half
⅛ teaspoon coarse red chili peppers
½ cup fresh basil

1 teaspoon Italian herb sprinkle
8 sliced sundried tomato garnish
⅓ cup black Moroccan olives, chopped for garnish
1 teaspoon sea salt
1 package Violife Parmesan, shredded
1 package Kite Hill Ricotta
1 tablespoon coconut oil for roasting
2 tablespoons olive oil

Preheat oven to 350°F. Grease a roasting pan with coconut oil, and add sliced potatoes, 2 red peppers, shallots, red onion, sweet onion, and 3 garlic cloves. Roast for 30 minutes.

In a large sauté pan, add olive oil, chopped red pepper, sliced garlic cloves, sliced basil, and zucchini noodles. Sauté on very low heat; you want to warm your noodles and ingredients together.

Once the vegetables are done roasting, in a large bowl add the noodles and roasted veggies. Sprinkle with Violife parmesan, add Kite Rill ricotta, and mix together.

Serve with sundried tomato and black olive garnish, with extra parmesan to taste.

Roasted Veggies and Potato

Lunch or Dinner—Better as a lunch option because it's heavier and will take longer to digest.

1 roasted onion
2 medium red bliss or blue potatoes, roasted
½ cauliflower, roasted
½ head broccoli, roasted
1 bunch fresh mint, chopped
1 bunch fresh basil, ribbon roasted
2 tablespoons coconut oil
1 teaspoon sea salt
⅛ teaspoon cracked pepper

Preheat oven to 350°F. Roast your veggies and potatoes in a large pan with coconut oil, sea salt, and cracked pepper for 35 minutes.

Slice potatoes in half-moons, slice cauliflower like fillets, cut broccoli into florets, and slice onion in half-moons.

Layer your salad: chopped greens first, then add radish around the bowl, then fresh herbs and olives, roasted veggies, potatoes, and onion on top. Garnish with sprouts.

Alkaline Umeboshi

Lunch or Dinner

⅓ cup umeboshi plum vinegar (Japanese vinegar), very alkaline
⅓ cup toasted sesame oil
⅛ teaspoon sea salt
⅛ teaspoon cracked pepper
⅛ teaspoon granulated kelp

Combine ingredients and shake well to mix. This lasts for weeks, even sitting on the countertop.

Cilantro Avocado Spice Cream
Lunch or Dinner

1 bunch cilantro

2 dates

1 cup coconut water

3 tablespoons avocado oil

½ jalapeño chili, fresh

1 avocado

1 garlic clove

1 tablespoon coconut amino

1 teaspoon sea salt

1 lime (juice only)

½ cup purified water, or as needed

Blend all ingredients in a high speed/powered blender.

Beautifying Detox Smoothie
Lunch or Dinner

1 cup wild blueberries, frozen (or 1 tablespoon wild blueberry
    powder from Anthony Williams)
1 cup coconut water
1–2 banana, frozen
1 teaspoon pure Hawaiian spirulina

Blend all ingredients at high speed until smooth. Enjoy!

Chocolate Fantasy Pie

Jeff and Helen Rose, Raw Food Chefs
Lunch or Dinner

Crust
1½ cup Natural Zing almonds
1½ cup Natural Zing dates, pitted

Filling
1 cup Natural Zing cacao nibs
½ cup Natural Zing coconut oil
½ cup Natural Zing cashews
½ cup Natural Zing agave nectar
1 Natural Zing vanilla bean

Crust
Blend nuts and dates in a food processor until well blended. Press into a pie plate to form a pie crust.

Filling
Blend nibs, coconut oil, cashews, and vanilla bean in a high-powered blender. Use a spatula to work mixture into the blade. As the mixture warms up, it will blend together.

Add agave and blend briefly until mixed. Pour into the crust, smoothing with a spatula. Refrigerate or freeze for 3 hours.

Lisa's Note: *Jeff Rose is the owner of Natural Zing, and Helen is the owner of Superfoods on Main (a vegetarian cafe in Mount Airy, Maryland).*

Greenest of Green Salad Dressing Recipe
Lunch or Dinner

½ cup organic lemon juice
½ cup olive oil, Bariani or Olio Beato brand
1 teaspoon Natural Zing Balinese stone-ground sea salt
2 tablespoon Natural Zing spirulina powder

Blend or shake all ingredients together well. Pour over any salad and enjoy the best salad ever!

Raw Cashew Cheese
Lunch or Dinner

Serves: 6–8

3 cups Natural Zing cashews, soaked
½ fresh red bell pepper
½ tablespoon Natural Zing red pepper
1 scallion
2 lemons, juiced
1 teaspoon dried rosemary (or 2 teaspoons fresh rosemary)
1 teaspoon Liquid Aminos or Nama Shoyu (or 1 teaspoon
    Celtic Sea Salt)

Soak cashews for 2 hours, then drain.

Place cashews and red bell pepper in a food processor with the liquid ingredients. Mix until smooth and place in a bowl.

Chop the red pepper and scallion, then mix with the cashew paste. Finely chop up the rosemary before adding the rosemary, lemon juice, and liquid aminos to the mixture.

Fold the rosemary into the cashew paste. Remove from bowl and serve with flax crackers.

Energy Smoothie Bowl

Lunch or Dinner

Filling
1 frozen banana
1 handful fresh baby spinach
¼ teaspoon Natural Zing Matcha green tea powder
1 teaspoon Natural Zing maca powder

Toppings
½ sliced banana
1 tablespoon Natural Zing cacao nibs
1 tablespoon cashew butter
1 handful fresh blueberries

Blend all filling ingredients in a high-speed blender. Pour into a bowl and add your toppings.

Chocolate Endurance Bowl

Lunch or Dinner

Filling
1 frozen banana
1 cup frozen strawberries
1 tablespoon Natural Zing cacao powder
1 teaspoon Natural Zing maca powder

Toppings
½ sliced banana
2 sliced strawberries
1 tablespoon Natural Zing coconut flakes
1 tablespoon Natural Zing cacao nibs

Blend all filling ingredients in a high-speed blender. Pour into a bowl and add your toppings.

Superfood Smoothie
Lunch or Dinner

Filling
1 frozen banana
1 cup frozen raspberries, strawberries, and blackberries
1 tablespoon Natural Zing chia seeds

Toppings
½ sliced banana
2 sliced strawberries
1 tablespoon gluten-free granola
1 tablespoon Natural Zing goji berries

Blend all filling in a high-speed blender. Pour into a bowl and add your toppings.

Protein Smoothie Bowl

Lunch or Dinner

Filling

1 frozen banana

1 cup rehydrated sliced Natural Zing mango

1 tablespoon Natural Zing pea protein powder

Toppings

½ sliced banana

2 tablespoons nut butter (peanut, almond, cashew)

1 tablespoon Natural Zing cacao nibs

Blend all filling ingredients in a high-speed blender. Pour into a bowl and add your toppings.

Walnut Fiesta Burrito

Jeff Rose, Owner of Natural Zing
Lunch or Dinner—Better as a lunch option because it's heavier and
will take longer to digest.

2 cups Natural Zing Walnuts, soaked
1 clove organic garlic
1 tablespoon Olio Beato olive oil
½ teaspoon organic chili powder
½ teaspoon organic cumin powder
½ teaspoon organic chipotle powder
2 tablespoons nama shoyu
3–4 fresh organic collard leaves

Soak walnuts overnight (or at least 8 hours) and drain. Place the
walnuts into a food processor and pulse until the walnuts reach a
taco filling-like texture. Pour into a bowl, add in all the remaining
ingredients, and mix gently to combine.

Spoon some of the filling out onto a collard leaf. Add whatever
fresh ingredients you like, such as tomatoes, avocado, and romaine.
Fold and enjoy.

Mung Bean Stew

Lunch or Dinner

This mung bean stew is super nourishing with healthy fats, protein-packed mung beans, and inflammation-fighting turmeric and black pepper.

2 grated carrots

2 celery stalks, diced

1 onion, diced

1½ cups soaked mung beans (sprouted is even better)

2 cans whole fat coconut milk

3 cups water

2 tablespoons grated ginger (more if desired)

1 teaspoon ground black pepper

2 tablespoons turmeric powder (or grated turmeric)

Celtic sea salt, to taste

Sauté the carrot, celery, and onion in a heavy pot. Add coconut milk, water, ginger, black pepper, turmeric, and sea salt. Let simmer until beans reach the desired texture. You may add more of the seasonings as desired. Serve with a mixed green salad.

Avocado Mousse with a Twist

Lunch or Dinner

This is an energizing treat—very versatile, it is a true superfood in a bowl. Maca is an adaptogen (it helps the body deal with stress and fatigue) and camu camu is an incredible bio-available source of vitamin C. These, mixed with the superfood qualities of the cacao and the healthy fats of the avocado, set you up for hours of energy!

1 avocado

1 banana

⅓ cup + 1 tablespoon real maple syrup

⅓ cup cacao powder

1½ teaspoon maca

1½ teaspoon camu camu

¼ cup cashew or almond milk

Add all of the ingredients to a high-power blender and blend. The milk measurement will depend on how thick you want your mousse; add until it has the consistency you want. Refrigerate for at least 1 hour before eating.

Cookie Dough Pumpkin Baked Oatmeal

Breakfast, Lunch or Dinner

Serves: 4-6

2 cups rolled oats

½ teaspoon sea salt

½–1 teaspoon pumpkin pie spice

⅓ cups pure maple syrup

1 (15 oz) can organic pumpkin puree

1–1½ cups nut milk of choice (I use unsweetened vanilla
    cashew milk)

2 tablespoon coconut oil (melted)

1 teaspoon pure vanilla extract

⅓ cup cacao nibs

Grease an 8 x 8 square pan. Preheat oven to 350°F.

In a large mixing bowl, stir together all dry ingredients. Add all remaining ingredients, starting with 1 cup of milk and adding more according to how it soaks into the dry ingredients. Stir in cacao nibs or sprinkle on top, if desired. Bake for 25 minutes, then turn off the heat and let sit in oven for 15 more minutes.

Top with an additional drizzle of maple syrup if desired. Enjoy!

Eggplant Bacon

Lunch or Dinner

You might want to double this recipe, because once you start eating it, you won't be able to stop! Eat it alone or on a salad as a garnish or sprinkled on top of roasted veggies.

1 medium eggplant
2 tablespoons extra virgin olive oil
1 teaspoon Bragg's liquid aminos or coconut aminos
1 teaspoon real maple syrup
½ teaspoon smoked paprika
Fresh ground pepper, to taste

Preheat oven to 300°F. Line two baking sheets with parchment paper.

Cut eggplant in half lengthwise, slicing each half into long, thin strips. In a small bowl, whisk together the olive oil, aminos, maple syrup, and paprika. Place the eggplant slices onto the baking sheets and brush both sides with sauce. Season with pepper.

Bake until eggplant is cooked through and beginning to get crisp, about 45–50 minutes.

Individual Vegan Apple Tart: Raspberry Sorbet and Meringue

From Chef Jamie Gardinor
Lunch or Dinner

Pastry
2 cups all purpose flour
1½ tablespoons castor sugar
¾ cup vegan margarine
½ tablespoon salt
3 tablespoons cold water
1½ tablespoons vegetable or
    olive oil
6 apples
½ cup dark brown sugar

Raspberry Sorbet
7 cups fresh or defrosted
    raspberries
1 cup water
1¼ cup sugar
Half a squeezed lemon

Vegan Meringue
7 tablespoons chickpea
    water (brine drained
    from a tin of chickpeas)
½ teaspoon cream of tartar
1 cup sieved icing sugar
½ teaspoon fruit puree
Pinch of salt

Pastry
Mix all dry ingredients in a large bowl. Add margarine in clumps and start to incorporate with the dry mix until flaky. In a separate bowl, whisk water and oil together and add to the mix, working until a non-sticky dough forms. Chill for 20–40 minutes, then roll to desired thickness (1/4-inch is best).

Preheat oven to 350°F. Grease a muffin tray, then cut circles out of the pastry and add to the tray, making sure it overlaps the edges (to compensate for shrinkage). Bake for 15–20 minutes. Remove and let cool. Once cooled, trim the edges for a more aesthetically pleasing tart.

Peel and quarter apples (removing the cores) and roll in soft dark brown sugar. In a pan on medium heat, add apples and slowly cook, adding some vegan margarine until the sugar has melted and the apples begin to soften. Put 3–4 pieces of apple in each base and top with extra brown sugar. Return to oven and bake for another 5–10 minutes.

Raspberry Sorbet
Put sugar and water in a pan and heat slowly until sugar is dissolved. Set aside and cool. Blend raspberries and lemon juice in a blender until very smooth; you may opt to pass it though a fine sieve for smoother texture. Combine both mixtures and add to an ice cream maker, following manufacturer's instructions.

Vegan Meringue
Add chickpea water to mixer and mix on high speed with cream of tartar and salt until it starts to foam, then add sugar a tablespoon at a time. Once the mixture has thickened, add desired fruit puree. Add mix to piping bag with any nozzle you fancy using.

Bake at 200°F for 55 minutes, then turn oven down to 125°F for 20 minutes, then turn off heat and let sit for 30 minutes.

Build your dish as you wish with fresh fruits. I find adding lemon balm makes for a nice extra touch!

THE RECIPES

Spiced Kuri Squash Soup

Lunch or Dinner—Works well as a dinner option, as it's lighter.

1 average-sized kuri squash
2–3 small potatoes, cut into
small chunks
1 small onion, chopped
3 cloves garlic, chopped
2 teaspoons curry powder
1 teaspoon ground
coriander

½ teaspoon ground ginger
¼ teaspoon dried thyme
1 (32 oz) carton vegetable
stock
Olive oil
Salt and pepper, to taste

Preheat the oven to 400°F.

Cut the squash in half and remove seeds and soft center. Drizzle with a little olive oil, sprinkle with salt and pepper and 1 chopped garlic clove, and place on a parchment-lined baking sheet, skin-side up. Roast for approximately 25 minutes. The skin will appear soft and pliable when punctured or pressed. Remove from oven and allow to cool.

While the squash is cooling, chop potatoes, onions, and garlic. To a soup pot, add a drizzle of olive oil and allow to heat. Add the potatoes, onions, garlic, salt, and pepper, and cook for a few minutes while stirring to coat. Add spices and herbs and continue to stir to coat.

Add stock and allow to cook for approximately 15–20 minutes to further soften the potatoes. While that is simmering, remove skin from the cooked squash and chop. Add to soup and allow to simmer for about 10 minutes more.

Ladle the soup into a food processor to blend together. If the soup gets too thick, thin it out with more stock or a little water.

You can substitute any type of squash or pumpkin for the kuri squash; kuri just happens to taste the best in this recipe!

Gandules Con Coco
(Green Pigeon Peas with Coconut)

From Jeesely Soto

Lunch or Dinner—Works well as a dinner option, as it's lighter.

1 (15 oz) can green pigeon peas (gandules verde)

1 teaspoon tomato paste

1 teaspoon adobo seasoning

½ teaspoon garlic powder

½ teaspoon onion powder

½ teaspoon dried cilantro

¼ teaspoons dried oregano

2 tablespoons chopped red pepper

½ teaspoon chopped garlic

½ cup water

1 (13.5 oz) can unsweetened coconut milk

Drain water from the can of beans and place in a sauce pan. Add seasonings and cook on medium-high heat for about 3–4 minutes to let the flavors absorb.

Add water and bring to a boil. Add coconut milk and bring to a boil again. Cover and cook on low-medium heat for 10 minutes. Uncover and cook for 5 more minutes. Serve over a bed of rice or quinoa.

Chocolate Berry Avocado Smoothie Bowl

From Jennifer Tolnay
Breakfast, Lunch or Dinner

Makes: 2 cups

1 avocado

3 cups spinach

1½ cups raspberries, strawberries, and/or cherries, fresh or
   thawed

2 tablespoons raw cacao powder

2 tablespoons pure maple syrup

¼ teaspoon vanilla

Combine all ingredients in a food processor and process until smooth. Transfer to bowls and top with any of the following: ground flax seed, hemp seeds, cacao nibs, more berries or cherries, or sliced bananas.

Quinoa Salad

From Jennifer Tolnay
Lunch or Dinner

Makes: 6 cups

1 cup uncooked quinoa (see note)
2 cups water
1 cucumber
1 red bell pepper
1 bunch scallions
3 tablespoons red wine vinegar
1 tablespoon extra virgin olive oil
1 tablespoon salt-free seasoning blend
1 teaspoon dill
Sea salt and pepper, to taste

Combine 1 cup quinoa and 2 cups water in a saucepan. Bring to a boil, reduce heat, and simmer for 15 minutes. Remove from heat and allow to stand covered for 5 minutes. Uncover and refrigerate until cold.

Chop cucumber and bell pepper and slice scallions. Once quinoa has cooled, combine with the vegetables. In a small bowl, whisk vinegar, oil, seasoning blend, and dill. Stir into quinoa and veggies mixture. Add salt and pepper to taste. Serve chilled or at room temperature.

If your quinoa isn't prewashed or sprouted, be sure to rinse thoroughly before cooking.

Lentil Vegetable Soup

From Jennifer Tolnay
Lunch or Dinner—Works well as a dinner option, as it's lighter.

12 cups vegetable broth
1 teaspoon grapeseed oil, optional
1 onion, chopped
2 cloves garlic, minced
4 carrots, sliced
1 yellow squash, cubed
1 zucchini, cubed
4 Yukon Gold potatoes, cubed
1 small (or ½ large) bunch curly kale, torn into bite-size pieces
1½ cups lentils, sorted and rinsed
1 bay leaf
1 tablespoon Italian seasoning
½ tablespoon basil
½ teaspoon turmeric
Salt and pepper, to taste

Sauté onion and garlic in oil until softened. For an oil-free soup, sauté in a little water or vegetable broth. Add carrots, squash, and zucchini and cook for 5 minutes, stirring to prevent sticking. Add lentils, potatoes, and spices. Bring to a boil, reduce heat, and simmer for 45 minutes or until lentils and potatoes are tender. Remove bay leaf. Stir in kale and cook until slightly wilted.

3 Mushroom Medley

From Chef Jenny Ross
Lunch or Dinner

4 cups cremini mushrooms
1 cup mitiake mushrooms, sliced
1 cup shitake mushrooms, sliced

For the Marinade:
¼ cup olive oil
2 tablespoons tamari (gluten-free)
1 tablespoon mellow white miso
1 teaspoon raw garlic or garlic powder

Combine the marinade ingredients using a personal blender. In a mid-sized mixing bowl, pour the marinade over the mushrooms, massaging the marinade into the mushroom fibers. Place the mixture in a cooking bag and vacuum seal. You may also use 16 oz mason jars, firmly packed.

Place the sealed bag or mason jars in a Tribest Sousvant and set the temperature to 118°F. Cook until the display shows an elapsed time of 4–6 hours. Serve as a side dish or enjoy as a light meal.

Corn Chowder

Lunch or Dinner—Works well as a dinner option, as it's lighter.

3 cups white corn

2 tablespoons nutritional yeast

¼ cup pine nuts

1 clove garlic or 1 teaspoon garlic salt

½ cup water

1 teaspoon chili powder

Blend all ingredients well in a personal blender. Place the mixture in a cooking bag and vacuum seal or use the displacement method for zip top bags. You may also use 16 oz mason jars, firmly packed.

Place the sealed bag or mason jars in a Tribest Sousvant and set the temperature to 118°F. Cook until the display shows an elapsed time of 4–5 hours.

Marinated Lotus Roots

From Chef Jenny Ross
Lunch or Dinner

2 cups raw lotus root, sliced to ¼ inch thick

For the marinade:
4 tablespoons sesame oil
4 tablespoons tamari
2 tablespoons sesame seeds
2 tablespoons raw agave chili spice, as desired

Mash garlic with a knife and spread the mashed garlic, salt, and pepper onto the chicken breasts. Place the chicken breasts into a cooking bag along with the lemon slices, rosemary, and olive oil. Vacuum seal the bag or use the displacement method for zip top bags.

Place the sealed bag in a Tribest Sousvant and set the temperature to 140°F. Cook until the display shows an elapsed time of 1 hour.

Once cooked, the chicken can be served immediately or seared on a stove or grill for 1–2 minutes on each side. Serve with vegetables or potatoes.

Pesto Vegetables

From Chef Jenny Ross
Lunch or Dinner

1 cup, shredded carrots
1 cup zucchini (cut into ½ moons, ¼ inch thick)
1 cup broccoli

For the marinade:
¼ cup olive oil
1 teaspoon lemon juice
¼ cup basil
2 cloves garlic
1 teaspoon sea salt

Blend the marinade ingredients in a personal blender until well combined. Place vegetables and marinade in a cooking bag and vacuum seal or use the displacement method for zip top bags.

Place the sealed bag in a Tribest Sousvant and set the temperature to 125°F. Cook until the display shows an elapsed time of 2–3 hours.

Shallot-Pistachio-Balsamic Brussels Sprouts

From Chef Joe Barr
Lunch or Dinner
If you eat this dish with something else, then serve at lunch time. If you want a light meal and are just eating these Brussels sprouts alone, then this is suitably light faire for dinner.

2 pounds Brussels sprouts, cleaned and halved
¼ cup shelled pistachios, roughly chopped
1 peeled shallot, diced
¼ cup aged balsamic vinegar
2 tablespoons + 1 tablespoon Evoo or avocado oil
Salt and pepper, to taste

Preheat oven to 375°F. Toss sprouts with 2 tablespoons oil and salt and pepper. Lay out on a sheet pan or cookie sheet and roast for 15–20 minutes, until golden in color and tender.

In a sauté pan over medium heat, add 1 tablespoon oil and chopped shallots. Once they are caramelized, add in chopped pistachios and toast for 1 minute. Mix shallot/pistachio mixture with roasted sprouts. Finish with aged balsamic and serve.

Cauliflower Stir Fry with Tofu

From Nancy Barr
Lunch or Dinner

1 large head cauliflower (about 4–5 cups of "rice")
3–4 spring onions, finely chopped (including green top)
4–5 medium mushrooms, sliced
6–8 small broccoli florets
1 red bell pepper, diced
¼ cup slivered carrots
2 cloves garlic, minced
1½-inch ginger, minced
1–1½ tablespoons oil (for stir fry)
1 pound tofu, drained and cubed

Sauce
4 tablespoons soy sauce
½ cup vegetable stock
½ teaspoon corn starch (may substitute with xanthan gum)

In a large non-stick skillet or wok, heat oil on medium heat. Add garlic and ginger and cook for approximately 10–15 seconds. Add broccoli and carrots and continue sautéing until broccoli starts turning a darker green. Add cauliflower, mushrooms, and tofu. Continue stir frying uncovered on medium heat, mixing frequently, until all vegetables are tender and the tofu is cooked through, approximately 10–15 minutes.

Meanwhile, prepare the sauce by whisking soy sauce, vegetable stock, and corn starch (or xanthan gum) together. Add the sauce and combine well to coat vegetables for a few minutes, until the sauce starts to thicken. Watch the heat during this process, turning it down if you notice it starting to stick to the pan. Add more vegetable stock to thin the sauce, if necessary. Add spring onions and continue cooking for another 1–2 minutes.

Build Your Own Vegan Bowl

From Olivia de Maigret
Lunch or Dinner
I've been addicted to bowls recently. For this recipe, you get to choose your grain, leaf, protein, and roasted veggies, building your own bowl any way you want!

Varies

Start with your base (grain), such as quinoa, wild rice, brown rice, farro, freekeh, or black rice. Add your greens, such as kale, spinach, watercress, or cabbage; your protein, such as any style of beans, tofu, shrimp, or salmon; any roasted vegetables you want, such as sweet potato, squash, broccoli, Bok choy, or bell pepper; and your toppings, including parsley, avocado, shredded carrots, watercress, peas, peanuts, egg, nuts/seeds.

And don't be afraid to add some pizzazz! Lemon juice, olive oil, pepper, salt, sesame oil, or rice vinegar can all transform your dish, giving it that extra something!

Vegan-Style Patty Up®

Lunch or Dinner—Better as a lunch option because it's heavier and will take longer to digest.

Serves: 4

2 tablespoons egg replacement
4 tablespoons + ¼ cup water
1 tablespoon oil
¾ cup firmly packed Patty Up® dry mix (one 3.38 oz bag)
¼ cup water
1 tablespoon tapioca starch flour
Coconut oil
Vegan cheese (optional)

Mix egg replacement, 4 tablespoons water, and oil together until smooth. Add Patty Up dry mix and remaining water and let set for 10 minutes. Form ¼ cup ball and flatten. Coat with 1 tablespoon tapioca starch flour and sauté in generous amount of coconut oil. Flip and finish, about 7 minutes. Top with vegan cheese or vegan sauces.

Shirley's Patty Up® Vegetarian Meat Balls with Sweet Red Sauce

Lunch or Dinner

Serves 4–6

Meat Balls
¾ cup firmly packed Patty Up® Burger Mix (or 1 packet)
3 tablespoons egg replacement
¼ cup panko bread crumbs
¼ cup water
1 tablespoon oil + extra for skillet
3 tablespoons grated vegan parmesan cheese
¼ cup fresh onion, minced
1 teaspoon parsley, dried
½ teaspoon salt

Sweet Red Sauce
1 cup ketchup
1 tablespoon horseradish sauce
½ cup brown sugar
1 tablespoon vinegar
Dash Worcestershire sauce

Combine all meat ball ingredients and let set for 10 minutes. The mixture will be slightly sticky and thin. Scoop with a cookie scooper or ⅛ cup measuring cup and sauté in generous amount of oil in a hot pan. Sauté each side until golden or bake at 375°F for 30–45 minutes.

Combine sweet red sauce ingredients in a pan and bring to a boil. Pour over meat balls and let simmer for another 5 minutes. Serve over your favorite pasta or rice.

Patty Up® Pancakes

Lunch or Dinner—Better as a lunch option because it's heavier and will take longer to digest.

Serves: 6–8

1 packet (or ¾ cup, firmly pressed) Patty Up® Burger Mix

4 tablespoons egg replacement

1 cup buttermilk

1¼ cups flour* (healthy option is coconut flour)

2 teaspoons baking soda

1 teaspoon salt

2 tablespoons sugar (healthy option is two dates, coconut sugar, or agave)

1 tablespoon oil + extra for skillet

Combine all ingredients and let set 5–10 minutes. Heat skillet over medium heat and coat pan with oil. Pour 1 cupful of batter onto skillet and cook until bubbles appear on the surface. Flip with spatula and cook until brown on other side. Serve with a dollop of butter. Drizzle with real maple syrup and sprinkle with powdered sugar.

* You can make this recipe gluten-free by using rice flour.

Shirley's Award Winning Meatless Chili

Lunch or Dinner—Better as a lunch option because it's heavier and will take longer to digest.

Serves: 8–10

2 packets (or 1½ cups) Patty Up® Burger Mix

4 tablespoons olive oil, divided

2 garlic cloves, minced very fine

1 cup diced scallions or onions

1 cup diced red fresh peppers

1 tablespoon chili powder

4 tablespoons Arriba Roasted Chipotle Salsa

1 (29 oz) can Petite cut diced chipotle chilies and tomatoes

1 (29 oz) can black beans

1 cup canned or frozen corn

1 teaspoon white pepper

2 teaspoons salt

1 cup sugar (or raw honey)

2 tablespoons refined virgin coconut oil

Sauté garlic and onions in 2 tablespoons oil. Add remaining ingredients (except coconut oil and Burger Mix). Simmer 10 minutes. While this is simmering, sauté the Burger Mixture in the coconut oil until lightly browned. Thin with water if needed. Drizzle 2 tablespoons olive oil over chili before serving. Garnish with grated sharp cheese, a dollop of sour cream, and chopped fresh cilantro.

Patty Up® with Beans, Rice and Veggies

Lunch or Dinner—Better as a lunch option because it's heavier and will take longer to digest.

Serves: 8–10

2 packets (or 1½ cups) Patty Up® Burger Mix
2 tablespoons oil
3 cloves minced garlic
2 cups chopped scallions or onions
2 cups chopped red fresh peppers
2 cups canned black beans, strained
1 teaspoon salt
½ teaspoon black pepper
2 cups rice, cooked
3 tablespoons fresh parsley, chopped
Black olives and red olives (optional)

Sauté garlic and onions in oil. Add beans, red peppers, and seasoning and set aside. Sauté Burger Mix until golden brown and crumbly. Add to sautéed veggies and spoon over rice. Garnish with parsley and olives.

A special thank you to my friend Brenda Hess for this recipe!

Smokey Mushroom Risotto
Lunch or Dinner

Serves: 2

1 cup arborio rice
1 cup vegetable stock
½ cup dried porcini mushrooms
Olive oil
1 small shallot
1 clove garlic
½ cup red wine (optional)
2 ounces Treeline Classic Aged Artisanal Treenut Cheese
Salt and pepper, to taste

Soak the dried mushrooms in the vegetable stock and keep hot.

In a heavy-bottomed saucepan, brown the shallot and garlic in the olive oil. Add the rice and cook until it is lightly toasted. If you want to include wine, add the wine and stir keeping at a gentle boil.

One ladle at a time, with the rice at a gentle boil, add vegetable stock and mushrooms to the saucepan so that the stock cooks into the rice. When the rice is al dente (about 18 minutes), make sure there is enough liquid (add water if necessary). Keep the rice boiling very gently.

Grate the Treeline cheese and stir it in. Turn off the heat and add salt to taste. Serve with ground pepper and top with additional grated cheese.

Coco Nori Raw Savory Wrap

Lunch or Dinner

1 Coco Nori Original wrap
¼ lime
½ avocado
1–2 cups of spinach
¼ cup shredded carrots

Place spinach and carrots in the middle of the wrap. Place sliced or mashed avocado on top of wrap and squeeze lime juice on top of ingredients. Wrap up and enjoy!

Spicy Vegan Wraps with Tangy Almond Sauce

Lunch or Dinner

1 Spicy WrawP
2 lettuce leaves
½ yellow bell pepper
⅛ red cabbage, finely chopped
¼ green onion
¼ Persian cucumber

Sauce
2 garlic cloves
2 cups chopped bell pepper (red, orange, or yellow)
2 tablespoon raw almond butter
1 tablespoon tamari
1 tablespoon lime juice
2 tablespoons coconut sugar
1 tablespoon chia seeds

For the sauce, blend all ingredients together in high speed blender until completely smooth.

Chop all vegetables. Place a dollop of sauce on the wrawp and spread on about a third of it. Place all the veggies on top of the sauce, wrap up, and enjoy!

Raw Traditional Pizza

Lunch or Dinner—Works better as a lunch option because it's heavier and will take longer to digest.

1 Original WrawP pizza crust
3 mushrooms, sliced
2 tablespoons sliced red onions
4 sliced olives
¼ cup of spinach

Sauce
2 tomatoes, chopped
4–5 dates
4–5 sun-dried tomatoes
2 cloves garlic, minced
1 capful olive oil
Oregano/basil

Blend all sauce ingredients together in a high-speed blender until smooth. Spread sauce on top of Original WrawP pizza crust. Add dash of oregano and basil on top of sauce. Place spinach on top of the sauce and top with mushrooms, red onions, and olives. Enjoy!

Roasted Red Pepper Cashew Dip

From Zoe Sakos

3 cups raw cashews

3 roasted red peppers

2 roasted garlic cloves

2 tablespoons olive oil

1 tablespoon nutritional yeast

2 teaspoons kosher salt

1 teaspoon white pepper

1 cup cold water

Soak the raw cashews in water for 30 minutes and drain. Roast red peppers over an open flame until skin is charred. Place in a closed paper bag for 10 minutes, then remove skin, stem, and seeds. Slow roast peeled garlic cloves in olive oil over low heat until golden brown.

Blend ingredients in a food processor while adding cold water to reach desired consistency. Serve with fresh vegetables and apple slices.

My Famous Stuffed Portobello Mushroom Caps

From Catherine Gill
Works better as a lunch option.

3 large Portobello mushroom caps
3 tablespoons extra-virgin olive oil
1 garlic clove, minced
¼ cup onion, finely chopped
2 tablespoons red bell pepper, finely chopped
⅛ cup celery, finely chopped
12 ounces vegan sausage, chopped
⅓ cup breadcrumbs
2 tablespoons vegan parmesan cheese, grated
2 tablespoons fresh parsley, chopped
1 tablespoon balsamic vinegar

Preheat oven to 400°F. Wash Portobello caps and remove stems; reserve stems and chop them finely. Rub mushroom caps with 1 tablespoon of olive oil and place on a greased baking sheet, stem-side up.

In a large skillet on medium heat, sauté garlic and onion in olive oil until fragrant. Add reserved mushroom stems, bell pepper, and celery, and sauté until tender. Add sausage and cook until brown. Remove from heat and mix in breadcrumbs, parmesan cheese, and parsley; divide mixture into Portobello caps and stuff them. Bake for about 15–20 minutes, or until tender and tops are golden brown.

Drizzle with balsamic vinegar before serving.

Crunchy Chickenless Salad

From Catherine Gill
Works as lunch or dinner option.

2 cups vegan chicken, cooked and cubed
½ cup celery, diced
1 small crisp apple, chopped
¼ onion, finely chopped
½ cup vegan mayonnaise
Salt and pepper, to taste

In a large mixing bowl, toss all ingredients together. Serve over a bed of lettuce or on toasted bread to enjoy as "chicken" salad sandwiches.

Split Pea Soup with Tempeh "Bacon"

From Catherine Gill
Works as a lunch or dinner option.

1 tablespoon olive oil
2 teaspoons vegan Worcestershire sauce
1 tablespoon maple syrup
1 tablespoon soy sauce
1 (8-ounce) package tempeh, thinly sliced
2 cups dried split peas
12 cups water
1 large onion, finely chopped
½ cup celery, finely chopped
1 teaspoon dried parsley
Black pepper, to taste
Salt and pepper, to taste

Preheat oven to 350°F. In a medium mixing bowl, combine olive oil, Worcestershire sauce, maple syrup, soy sauce, and black pepper; toss tempeh slices in sauce mixture and coat well. Arrange tempeh evenly in a greased baking pan and drizzle with any remaining sauce. Bake for 20 minutes, turning once halfway through; "bacon" is done when crispy and browned.

In a large stockpot, bring split peas and water to a gentle boil, and continue to boil for 5 minutes. Add onion, celery, and parsley to soup; cover and simmer for 1 hour or until split peas are tender and liquid is partially reduced. Serve with tempeh "bacon" crumbled on top.

Maple Glazed Carrots

From Catherine Gill
Works better as a lunch item.

3 tablespoons vegan butter
½ small onion, chopped
1 teaspoon dried parsley
8 medium carrots, peeled and quartered
¼ cup vegetable stock
¼ cup maple syrup

In a large frying pan on medium heat, melt butter and sauté onion and parsley until onion is tender. Stir carrots and maple syrup in pan; reduce heat to medium-low. Cover and cook until carrots are tender, stirring occasionally.

CONCLUSION

I continue to read that if you live a healthy lifestyle, your odds of avoiding all the big diseases caused by poor diet and lifestyle are eighty percent better. Plus, it you *do* get something, your odds are eighty percent better that you will beat it.

My mom was diagnosed with diabetes in 1995. It wasn't really a surprise; all the female members of her family got diabetes. When she was in the hospital trying to stabilize her diabetes and setting up a corrective diet plan (that she didn't stick to), I asked her endocrinologist what I could do to make sure I didn't get diabetes (since there was a genetic predisposition). He told me to keep doing what I was doing—eating healthy and exercising. As part of my annual physicals, they test my blood sugar, and I still show no signs of diabetes. Even if something seems like a given—such as a genetic predisposition for diabetes—that's no reason to give up without a fight! All that does is set you up for failure.

By taking control of your life—your mind, body, and spirit, your finances, your emotional development—you empower yourself and give yourself the freedom to live your life as you choose, instead of being stuck in a wheelchair, sick and broken. Don't stay with a rotten job just because you ran up debt. Believe me, I know that it takes time to pay off that mortgage and work through your emotional development. Exercise and eating healthy can strengthen your body, better enabling you to persevere and put in the effort to find your own blissful freedom.

As I'm writing this book, David Cassidy of Partridge Family fame has just passed. And do you know what his last words were, per his daughter?

"So much wasted time."

So don't waste any more time. Take control of your life and make today the best day ever. You can do this. You are worth it. You get one chance at this life and it goes by very quickly.

Make it count and live dynamically!

ACKNOWLEDGMENTS

Throughout my writing journey, my books have tended to be dedicated to people—loved ones who have impacted my life significantly and who have passed. Now I'm almost afraid to say any one person, as I don't want to jinx them if they are alive!

Therefore, this book is dedicated to those who have helped me grow as a person, whether knowingly or unknowingly. I feel so blessed for the cheerleaders/friends who love me, and who support me through the good, bad, and ugly. Thank you, I love you.

But our biggest periods of growth aren't necessarily from the happy times in our life, or due to our cheerleaders. For me, ironically, the biggest growth has come from the challenges and the dastardly people I've met along the way, whether it be family members, ex-spouses, or bosses. Let's be real—if I hadn't developed food allergies and candida, which was a big challenge and a huge learning journey for me, I wouldn't have written nine books. So now, whenever challenging times come, I look for how I can learn and/or grow from it. And the neat thing is, even when the challenging times come, I still feel joy and peace in my heart. Look back and reflect on all the challenging times in your life and remember that you have come through them all. Own that growth; be proud of who you have become. You *are* good enough—more than good enough!

It took me a long time to come into my own. I felt like I had to go through many challenging experiences, all so that I would grow, learn, and be able to relate to the challenges other people who come into my life are going through.

We are here to support each other through the good times and the challenging times. A word, a smile can make all the difference in the world.

So thank you to all of my friends who have been so gracious to share their passion and their recipes. You don't have to be a health food expert (or even a raw food chef) to live this lifestyle. You can be a teenager going to high school; a purchasing agent buying millions of goods for your company; a teacher; a mom or dad.

Special thanks to the folks at Hatherleigh Press and Penguin Random House, who continue to support my prayer to make a difference and to be used by God. Thank you to Martin Pearl Publishing, who published my first book, *Raw Inspiration*.

—LISA MONTGOMERY

Special, heartfelt thanks to those who took the time to share their stories, recipes, printing, art skills, editing, layout, and computer skills:

Heidi Albertsen: International Supermodel, actress, spokesperson, good will ambassador, Miss Universe judge

Josh Batman: My Rent-A-Son, special thanks for your computer skills

Nancy Barr: Entrepreneur

Chef Joe Barr

Anglina Ritter (Just Vegan)

Brenda Hinton (Rawsome Creations)

Carolyn Wojton: Graphic designer, certified fitness and nutrition coach

Drs. Allison and Matt Lapp (Kimberton Wellness)

Phoenixville Veg Fest

Jeesely Soto: Co-founder

Ann Murphy: Co-founder

Zoe Sakos: Co-founder

Jennifer Tolmay: Former Committee member

Helen and Jeff Rose (Natural Zing)

Chef Jamie Gardiner

Catherine Gill, "The Dirty Vegan"

Awesome Foods

Olivia Demaigret

Janice Innella: The Original Beauty Chef

Jenny Ross (Tribest)

Tribest Corporation

Shirley Burns (Patty Up)

Treeline (Nut) Cheese

WrawP

Martin Pearl Publishing

Hatherleigh Press

Penguin Random House

MEET THE *VEGAN CHALLENGE* CONTRIBUTORS

HEIDI ALBERTSEN

Mom, Entrepreneur, International Model/Actress, Goodwill Ambassador, Humanitarian.

Heidi Albetsen is a Danish/American model and tv personality who now lives abroad. She was born in Copenhagen, Denmark, and is outspoken about the various health issues that she has faced throughout her life. Overweight as a girl, which led to her being subjected to ridicule, Heidi was inspired to lose the weight and pursue a healthy lifestyle, one that supported her body and spirit and helped her reach fame and fortune.

JENNY ROSS

Jenny Ross is a five-time Hay House best-selling author and wellness expert, is a passionate global educator. She also serves as president of the International Raw Foods association and staff Chef for Tribest International. Jenny's goal is to help others find their best health through foods that heal the body. Her work for the past two decades as a plant-based restaurant operator (118 Degrees) has made her a much sought-after chef and global resource in helping others get started in wellness food service. Find her online at facebook/jennyrosslivingfoods or on Instagram @jennrossrawfood.

Ann Murphy

A mother and certified Holistic Health Coach/Wellness Educator, Ann Murphy knows what it is like to live with chronic health issues. After doctors couldn't help her, she started on a journey of self-education and experimentation that resulted in great improvement to her health and life.

After attending the Institute for Integrative Nutrition, studying additional digestion courses, the psychology of eating, and the effects of environmental toxins, Ann pulled together everything she'd learned in ways that enabled her to help others make improvements in their health, energy levels, mindset, cravings, and weight.

Ann loves to help men and women get off the rollercoaster of diets, DVDs, books, and programs based on restriction and deprivation. Having learned that everyone is different and that there is no "right" way to success in weight loss or health, she'll tell people: "If you're ready to stop listening to everyone else and listen to the only true expert on your body—YOU—I can help you!"

Email her at ann@newapproachwellness or check out her website, www.newapproachwellness.com.

Awesome Foods

Bruce and Marsha R. Weinstein are the creators, owners, and operators of Awesome Foods. Their passion for clean and healthy food is what led them to incorporate more raw foods into their diet.

As owners of a Natural Market since 1992, their desire to help people make better food choices has remained their mission for over 25 years. Inspired to help others create high-quality meals and snacks that are minimally processed, easy to digest, and taste awesome, they started Awesome Foods in September 2005 in a small commercial kitchen, with the goal of providing delicious raw, organic, gluten-free food to the public. In March 2017, they moved their kitchen to a much larger facility to better serve a growing demand.

Their mission is to revolutionize the way people eat by offering high quality prepared meals and snacks and by educating consumers, so individuals like you can make better dietary choices. After all, food is powerful medicine!

CAROLYN WOJTON

Carolyn Wojton's passion for food started at a very young age with the teachings of her Italian grandmother, who taught her many of the traditional Italian dishes, as well as the peasant style of cooking where you waste nothing and create beautiful, tasteful dishes from what others deem "food scraps."

Fast forward to the early 2000s, and Carolyn was diagnosed with celiac disease. Suddenly, all the knowledge from Grandmom Rose had to be adapted to use new ingredients and new cooking methods. It was through extensive research and her friendship with Lisa Montgomery that her eyes were opened to a new realm of nutrition and eating.

The next awakening came in 2017 via the natural age progression for women and an introduction to acupuncture. Carolyn's eyes were opened yet again to the dangers of inflammation and ways to eliminate it, as well as ways to eat more holistically to create a life-changing metamorphosis. She is beyond grateful for this path and the people she met along the way who helped to open her eyes and create a wonderful marriage between nutrition and fitness.

DRS. MATT AND ALLISON LAPP (KIMBERTON WELLNESS)

Drs. Matt and Allison Lapp practice an advanced form of chiropractic care called Network Spinal Analysis. Their philosophy is that the body has an innate intelligence that wants us to thrive and achieve a state of harmony. On a regular basis, they speak to individuals in their practice about diet and its impact on not only our health, but overall wellbeing. With so many choices, fads, and gimmicks available, it is easy to become overwhelmed. As practitioners, Matt and Allison do their best to encourage others to eat live, whole, organic foods whenever possible.

Elena Semenova

Growing up on a farm, Elena Semenova had organic fruits and vegetables readily available. Growing up with such a diet, she saw the value and importance of a healthy, raw, vegan diet and its positive effects for the body.

After moving to Los Angeles, she found it was nearly impossible to continue this diet. Dissatisfied with the products available on the market, as she felt the negative effects of consuming products outside her previous clean and healthy diet, Elena began to study nutrition and purchased fruits and vegetables from local farmers' markets.

With the addition of superfood spices, Elena created the original veggie WrawP out of necessity, to help her pursue her healthy lifestyle once more. After sharing it with family and friends, who loved it, she brought WrawP to local farmers' markets to share with the world. It was at one of these farmers' markets that she met Kraig Doorman, who fell in love with the product's taste and its positive effects on his body. Kraig quickly jumped on board and became a partner with Elena to help bring WrawP to life in 2012. Their mission is to supply a healthy, clean and delicious product to help anyone on any diet pursue a healthier lifestyle in a quick and easy way!

JANICE INELLA

The original Beauty Chef, it was while on a journey to wellness, beauty, and spiritual awakening that Janice was led toward living a vibrant life. Janice's healing journey started early on in her thirties, when she began having issues digesting baked carbohydrates. Still desiring to having her daily bread, she was faced with the limited choices available in the late 80s and early 90s for wheat-free bread replacements.

Everyone likes feeling good—being energetic, full of inspiration, with glowing skin, a trim waistline, and love in your heart. For Janice, that meant eating healthier, going for walks, and attending consistent yoga classes while learning to deal with stress. These are the kind of side effects you want from a consistent lifestyle change with food and healthy choices. Fortunately, with all her education about food health and beauty, Janice knows what to do to improve the quality and beauty in life.

JEESELY SOTO

Jeesely Soto has been vegan since 2012. In 2011, she came across an ad in her local newspaper for a program called the Phoenixville Vegan Pledge, a program which challenged the participants to go vegan for 30 days. Jeesely encouraged her husband to try it out, since he had recently been diagnosed as being pre-diabetic. At the time, she thought he would do it and then go back to eating meat again--and indeed, that was his plan--but in the end, he'd learned so much about being vegan that he decided to stay vegan. A few months later, Jeesely and their child became vegetarian, with their child transitioning to vegan not long afterwards.

In the last ten years, Jeesely's hometown has become popular for its growing list of festivals (such as BlobFest and the Firebird Festival). So she and two other friends decided to start a vegan food festival in their town, and the Phoenix-ville VegFest was born! With 3,000 visitors the first year, the festival has only continued to grow.

Jeesely describes herself as a foodie at heart, and that hasn't changed since becoming vegan. When she became vegan, she started taking her favorite Latin recipes and learning how to veganize them.

OLIVIA DE MAIGRET

Olivia was born and raised in the beautiful Napa Valley. Growing up, her parents made sure that eating healthy food was a priority for both Olivia and her sibling. But in middle school, Olivia started eating unhealthy foods, completely unaware of what she was doing to her body. She became moody, depressed, and very insecure; she was not a happy person and hated how she felt.

Then, during seventh grade, her mother took her to Ubud, Bali, where Olivia met the healthiest, most well balanced people she has ever known—Lisa Montgomery and Brenda Hilton.

After hearing them speak about their vegan lifestyle and how it helped them through their medical issues and life in general, Olivia understood that eating the right food is so important, and that our bodies and souls deserve better.

Olivia decided to change for the better, and when she arrived back home, she started eating clean and healthy, while incorporating exercise into her daily routine. A year later, for her eighth grade presentation, she chose to talk about "Vegan Cuisine." A pescatarian, Olivia holds a deep love for animals and our environment. Fast forwarding to the present, Olivia (now a junior in high school) has cultivated a genuine appreciation for healthy food and exercise (especially running). She is an overall more contented person, taking great pride in her healthy lifestyle. She hopes that through her journey she can inspire friends, family, and teachers to live a healthier lifestyle, and wants everyone to remember to love themselves because you are beautiful!

SHIRLEY BURRIS (PATTY UP)

Shirley Burris grew up on a farm where her family sold fruits and vegetables at a roadside produce stand, later to become Stauffer's of Kissel Hill, Lancaster County, Pennsylvania. When she was three years old, her father died at the young age of 47, leaving behind 11 children, and the fruit and vegetable farm became how her mother continued to support their family.

It was through the experiences growing natural food—food that is home-grown and eaten immediately—that led to Shirley creating foods to market through Burris Country Kitchen. She is working to create real food, and finds it very rewarding to work together with a team of people doing something that she loves.

Her main objective in creating Patty Up was to make a meat alternative with superior ingredients that tastes delicious, but which would (more importantly) help to eliminate all the excessive packaging and branding you find in grocery stores today. Patty Up is one product that can create hundreds of recipes. It is made from premium and pure ingredients without preservatives or chemicals. It is a no-fuss nutritious meal that provides not only taste, but is packed full of powerful nutrients and can be prepared to please vegans, vegetarians, and meat eaters alike. Visit Shirley's website at www.burriscountrykitchen.com for recipes.

MICHAEL SCHWARZ (TREELINE)

Treeline was born in the kitchen of its founder, Michael Schwarz, but it has its origins in Johannesburg, South Africa, where he grew up. Prior to starting

Treeline, Michael had run an international law practice in New York, which required frequent travel to Europe. There he sampled, and grew to love, fine French and Italian cheeses. Michael's parents had been prominent anti-apartheid activists in South Africa. They instilled in him the belief that you don't have to go along with something you know to be wrong, just because everyone else is doing it. Treeline was founded out of Michael's belief that the dairy industry, and thus cheese, is inherently unjust, and that the best way to fight that injustice is to provide a delicious alternative.

He set about creating a vegan cheese that is as good as the best cheeses he had enjoyed in France and Italy *and* is cruelty-free. Treeline cheeses are made with the simplest, purest ingredients—cashew nuts, probiotics, and herbs—and cultured to perfection. They are free of lactose, casein, soy, gluten, and added oils. From their humble beginnings in Michael's kitchen, Treeline cheeses can now be found in thousands of supermarkets, health food stores, and food co-ops nationwide.

ZOE SAKOS

Zoe Sakos has been leading a plant-based lifestyle for the past seven years. Growing up in the heart of Amish Country in Lancaster, PA, Zoe's childhood was filled with scrapple, chicken pot pie, and pig's stomach; now, she can't even fathom the thought of consuming those foods. Zoe first started to question eating meat during the Michael Vick controversy. This opened her eyes to the horrors of animal abuse and factory farming, leading her to adopt a vegetarian lifestyle, which quickly became vegan when she realized the dairy industry is just as cruel and destructive as the meat industry. While she enjoys the undeniable health benefits of a plant-based lifestyle, she continues to live vegan because her moral compassion is more important than her palate. When people ask her what she eats, she is happy to help them discover the amazing variety of foods available while still eating cruelty-free. She only wishes she'd made the change sooner!

CATHERINE GILL

Catherine Gill is a writer, blogger, and holistic vegan chef who specializes in natural and health foods. She studied and found her passion in writing, literature, and social science in college. She has run the popular blog The Dirty Vegan since 2010, focusing on comfort-food-style vegan recipes that are fun, accessible, and healthy. Author of *The Dirty Vegan Cookbook*, she also ran Dirty Vegan Foods, a vegan bakery specializing in veganized versions of classic desserts. She has an active social media presence with over 26K followers on twitter (@TheDirtyVegan). She currently resides in New England with her husband, daughter, and rescue dog.

RESOURCES

BOOKS

There are a number of books, classes, and workshops on vegan food and its benefits:

Food Can Fix It by Dr. Mehmet Oz

Rocco's Healthy & Delicious by Rocco Eispirito

Vegan Under Pressure by Jill Nussinow, MS, RDN. These are perfect vegan meals that you can make quickly and easily in a pressure cooker.

Vegan Pressure Cooking by J L Fields. Delicious beans, grains, and one-pot meals in minutes.

Rawsome Creations Nut Milk Bag Recipe Collection by Brenda Hinton

The Raw Revolution Diet by Cherie Soria, Brenda Davis, and Vesanto Melina

Raw Food Made Easy, Revised Edition by Jenny Cornbleet

The Raw 50 by Carol Alt

The Wheatgrass Book by Ann Wigmore. Ann Wigmore was one of the first people to bring wheatgrass and raw foods to the forefront.

Wheatgrass: Nature's Finest Medicine by Steve Myerowitz. I had the pleasure of meeting and learning from Steve Myerowitz, and considered him a friend. The first time I met him at a trade show, I was still a newbie in the healthy living field and I felt like I was meeting a rock star. Years later, we worked together at trade shows. After his passing, Steve's sons have continued his legacy of sharing healthy living via wheatgrass and sprouts.

The Body Ecology Diet: Recovering Your Health & Rebuilding Your Immunity by Donna Gates with Linda Schatz. My homeopath recommended this book to me in my early years of trying to build up my immune system, after being beaten down by the overgrowth of candida and eating food that I was allergic to. It's a good book for people with weakened immune systems as a result of candida, AIDS, cancer, chronic fatigue, and other immune disorders.

The Allergy Self-Help Cookbook by Margorie Hurt Jones, R.N. This book was so helpful to me in the early years of trying to find my way with food allergies. Before I started to create my own healthy recipes, I needed help learning to substitute new ingredients that I never had heard of or used before.

EQUIPMENT

Tribest Dynapro High-Power Commercial Vacuum Blender

The Tribest Dynapro high-power vacuum blender is the best commercially-certified high-speed blender for blending your favorite smoothies, soups, sauces, salsas, and more. This blender features innovative vacuum technology that allows you to remove excess air and oxygen inside the carafe before blending to protect your food from the oxidation that occurs in traditional high-speed blending. The Dynapro includes an easy one touch vacuum pump to ensure a tight vacuum seal which ensures the nutritional quality of the food, protecting it as you blend and providing you with a superior blend offering improved taste, texture, and shelf life This system protects the nutrient density of your blends and is simple to use, offering a 2.5 hsp motor and a 15 year warranty for home use.

Tribest Sousvant

The Sousvant is sous vide made simple! This is the easiest way to bring the gourmet culinary technique into the comfort of your own kitchen. The Tribest Sousvant guarantees precision temperature control of your food product to 1/10th of a degree by circulating the self -contained water bath from two points in the all enclosed system. The ease of use of all-in-one water ovens is exceeded with the Sousvant, because with this model you can easily see your foods working in the water bath and you can rely on the digital control panel to control the temperatures. This means there is no overcooking—you get perfect results every time! Foods are cooked thoroughly, flavors are intensified and foods are made healthier as a result of this low slow cooking method.

About five years ago, a world-renowned chef told me the biggest breakthrough for the vegan and raw world was utilizing the sous vide. He had used them to cook standard American fare, but when he utilized them in the vegan and/or raw world, it just took the plant-based food to a whole new, incredibly tantalizing level.

Tribest's Glass Personal Blender

Tribest's glass personal blender with variable speed dial and pulse function includes an 8 oz., 16 oz., and 24 oz. glass containers, as well as a storage lid and two travel lids. The components of this blender are all glass, stainless steel, and silicone, ensuring your food product never contacts any plastics. This is true clean blending! This blender is also available with a 42 oz glass vacuum container, allowing you to benefit from vacuum blending technology with a personal blender. The durability of the blade ensures you will be able to use the same blade for

years! This blender is a must-have for me, meeting both my kitchen and travel needs. If you want to make a small batch of baby food, salad dressing, smoothies, you name it—you can just pull out your personal blender.

A lighter-weight, more compact personal blender from Tribest is also available if you are just testing the waters. This unit features BPA-free plastic grab and go blending carafes, and it also has mason jar adaptability that is compatible with most standard mouth-sized mason jars, so you can blend, store, and drink out of your favorite and/or existing jars, making clean up super easy.

TRIBEST SLOWSTAR VERTICAL SLOW JUICER AND MINCER

Tribest's Slowstar is a vertical slow juicer and mincer with single auger cold press for extracting quality juice from your favorite fruits, vegetables and leafy greens. The Slowstar is a masticating juicer, it can easily juice things like wheatgrass as well.

When I first started juicing, my juicer could only do hard vegetables; I had to buy another juicer to do the leafy vegetables and soft fruits. How annoying! The Slowstar allows me to do it all, and because of the low speed, the juice stays fresher for longer and retains its nutritional quality. Another side benefit is it operates quietly and is a more affordable option when compared to pricier units using other juicing technology. I use the mincer attachment when I need to process a lot of onions or when I need to prepare a lot of cabbage/vegetables for raw sauerkraut.

TRIBEST GREENSTAR ELITE COLD PRESS COMPLETE MASTICATING JUICER

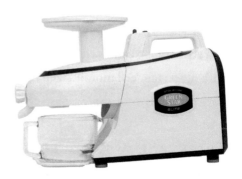

I start every day with my Tribest Greenstar Elite when I juice my wheatgrass. The primary technology in this slow horizontal juice press is the advanced jumbo twin gears, it gives you the most nutrients and juice-yield from your produce. The bio-ceramic magnetic core of the gear works to restructure the juice, allowing for three days of enzyme and nutrient activity in your fresh juices. You will also see greater juice yield due to the masticating twin gears pushing out all available liquids.

In my early years, my first juicer had to run the pulp through multiple times before I could get all the juice out. Not only was it annoying doing that at 6 a.m. but it overheated the pulp. With the Greenstar Elite, you run the fruit/vegetables once and it extracts all the juice the first time through. It's the only juicer that has a three-stage masticating system, which means it slices, cuts, and chews just like your teeth. The complete masticating design mimics the way nature intended our foods to be broken down at the beginning of the digestive process, so even though it is difficult to try and literally eat pounds of fruits, vegetables and greens in one sitting, you can still reap the benefits of drinking their nutrient-concentrated juices.

NUT MILK BAG

My search for a nut milk bag to meets my needs was finally over when I started using Rawsome Creations' Nut Milk Bag. These bags are designed by Brenda Hinton of Rawsome Creations and handmade in Bali, Indonesia, with part of the proceeds going to help to support Ibu Robinat Yayasan Bumi Sehat Birthing Center and the Yayasan Widya Guna Orphanage.

You can purchase Rawsome Creations Nut Milk bags directly from their web site (www.rawsomecreations.com) or through a major online distributor like Amazon.

Vitamix High-Powered Blender

The Vitamix has a 2.2 horsepower motor and a 5–7-year warranty. I bought my first Vitamix twenty years ago, and it is still going strong. Consumer Report continues to rate the Vitamix as the #1 blender in its class. Vitamix has consistently kept its quality standards high, but has also added options to keep current with the market, including numerous color choices and a lower-profile option to fit on your counter. They also recently lowered the number of years of their warranty, so as to lower overall costs and make it more affordable to more consumers.

Spiralizer

When I changed my diet thirty years ago, the only people using spiralizers were raw foodies. Now it seems everyone is catching on to how great these things can be. Spiralizers spiralize veggies such as squash (butternut, yellow, and green), zucchini, and red beets. Besides being great as a pasta/spaghetti substitute, spiralized veggies add different flavors and textures to salads, side dishes, and main courses. I even use spiralized vegetables when I make my raw sauerkraut.

Spiralized vegetables can be eaten cooked or raw. (Don't worry: even if you don't own a spiralizer, these days grocery stores have prepackaged fresh spiralized vegetables for sale.)

INSTANT PROGRAMMABLE PRESSURE COOKER, SLOW COOKER, STEAMER, SAUTÉ, YOGURT MAKER AND WARMER

The Instant Pot is currently the "in" piece of equipment for the vegan and/or the person on the go. It's great for making soups, stews, beans, and rice. You can sauté and steam your vegetables and pressure cook your rice.

RECIPE INDEX